MICHAEL GOINGS

Free at last?

THE REALITY OF RACISM IN THE CHURCH

God's Life
PUBLISHING

Free At Last? The Reality of Racism In The Church

Published by God's Life Publishing
NEW JERSEY HAWAII
744 Chancellor Avenue 4998C E. Ehiku Way
Irvington, New Jersey 07111 Ewa Beach, Hawaii 96706
email:godlife@aol.com www.godslifepublishing.org

This book or parts thereof may not be reproduced in any form, stored in a retrieval system, or transmitted in any form by any means—electronic, mechanical, photocopy, recording, or otherwise for commercial gain or profit—without prior written permission of the publisher. The use of short quotations or occasional page copying for personal or group study is permitted and encourage.

Unless otherwise identified, Scripture quotations are from the King James Version of the Bible.

Take note that the name satan and related names are not capitalized. We choose not to acknowledge him, even to the point of violating grammatical rules.

Cover design by God's Life Publishing

Art Director: Bishop Calvin L. Bethea

Copyright ©1995 by Michael Goings
All rights reserved
Library of Congress Cataloging-in-Publication Data: 2011925314
International Standard Book Number: 978-0-9916263-4-2
E-book ISBN: 978-0-9916263-3-5
Printed in the United States of America

Table Of Contents

Foreword V

Introduction VII

Chapter 1   Are We Salt and Light 1

Chapter 2   Defining the Disease of Racism 7

Chapter 3   The Roots of Racism 15

Chapter 4   The Reality of Racism In The Church 25

Chapter 5   The Consequences and Detriment of Racism in Christendom 37

Chapter 6   Rightly Dividing the Curse of Ham 45

Chapter 7   Am I Black or White by Chance or Divine Determination 49

Chapter 8   Interracial Marriages in the Church: Are They Scripturally Consistent 57

Chapter 9   True Confessions of a Once Racist Black Man 71

Chapter 10   Prophecy Demands the Defeat of Racism In The Church Before the Return of Jesus 79

Chapter 11   The Balm Of Gilead: The Only Cure for Racism is The Church 87

Final Words 105

End Notes 107

Foreword

There was a time when God overlooked our childish weaknesses, but now He is commanding men everywhere to repent (see Acts 17:30).

God raised up many of these voices here on the eastern coast of the Carolinas. One of these watchmen is my friend and ministerial colleague, Pastor Michael Goings of Dillon, South Carolina. He and his wife Louise have developed an effective prophetic ministry team that has impacted their surrounding locale. I have been in their home and preached in their local church, and know their ministry to be marked by purity, power, and practicality.

His life, education, and ministerial experience have equipped Pastor Goings to write the treatise now set before you: *Free at Last? The Reality of Racism in the Church*. This word from the Lord needs to be proclaimed in the ears of God's people everywhere, especially among his leaders.

The present reality of the Kingdom of God is the extension of God's rule or dominion throughout the earth and the universe. The Church, the Body of Christ, is the instrument of His government, called to be salt and light (see Matthew 5:13-16). Once he establishes this introductory truth, Pastor Goings then defines and classifies racism, explaining its root system. After the foundations of this awful ignorance are brought to light, this literary prophet then takes the reader on a journey through the Old and New Testaments to show the reality of racism in the Church.

He follows this by examining American history to corroborate and illustrate his main point.

Pastor Goings goes on to address many practical side issues. Was Ham "Cursed'? Is race determined by chance or divine determination? Are interracial marriages scriptural? These pragmatic sections are highlighted by the openness and honesty of this man of God as he shares his own testimony of being brought from a life of confrontation in Adam to his new life of emancipation in Christ.

This volume ends with a powerful one-two punch. First, we learn that the prophetic Scriptures demand the defeat and demise of racism before the literal return of Jesus Christ to this planet (see Ephesians 4:13; Hebrews 10:12-13). Second, we are given 12 dynamics that will work in our homes, schools, and churches to expose and eliminate racism.

Jesus Christ died for all men. We are all one in Him. *Free at Last? The Reality of Racism in the Church* is a tool in hand of the Lord to bring about His consummate purposes for America and the nations. We have entered the Feast of Tabernacles, a time of global harvest, the joy of the Lord, the appearing of the Lord in His people, and the unity of the faith.

This is not the day of the black man or the white man. It is the day of the "new Man," the Day of the Lord, and His Church! Thank you, Michael, for this most timely volume. We are indebted to you for these concepts and your convictions, but most of all, for your courage. I stand with you, brother.

> Pastor Kelley Varner, D.D., Th.D.
> Praise Tabernacle, Richlands, North Carolina

Introduction

Ever since the fall of man in the Garden of Eden, sin has permeated ever aspect of our life. The Prophet Jeremiah asked a most profound question,

> "Can the Ethiopian change his skin, or the leopard his spots? Then may ye also do good, that are accustomed to do evil" (Jeremiah 13:23).

Jeremiah was making it clear that there is some things no man can change about his physical features, but the power of the gospel can change our evil nature to a godly nature.

This change through Christ, renews our mind, change our vile heart, and causes us to see all men in the image of Christ (See Romans 12:1-2). Some in the Christian community have been negligent in internalizing the transforming power of Christ to make us new creatures (See 2 Corinthians 5:17). Professing Christians who lack this transformation are afraid or apathetic to acknowledge that they are infected with the deadly virus of racism.

Racism is not just a Caucasian and African-American conflict, but also a widespread misconception whereby one group feel superior to another group. Fearful that their job may be taken, increase competition for their women and their neighborhood transformed, the dominant group often feels threatened by the presence of the minority group. Anything that they believe should be exclusively theirs that seems as if they have to share causes great anxiety. As a result, the minority group may be ostracized on the job and sadly to say even in the Church. Though they only came to Church for Christ and fellowship, they are made to feel unwelcome. Recent research has revealed an alarming resurgence of racism in America and in the Church. The focus of this book is the discernment and removal of racism in the Bride of Christ.

I will use some of my first hand experiences to demonstrate the need to eradicate racism in the Church. In many ways, I have been preparing to write this book all of my life. First as a victim, and then as a promoter of racism. I have acquired extensive practical knowledge on the matter from both sides. As a result of being born with a sin nature, I was held captive by the powers of racism and bigotry from the time of my natural birth to the moment of my spiritual rebirth. Born into a system of segregation and discrimination, I lived in the valley of the disadvantaged and oppressed. The devil and the world told me it was because of my color and ethnicity.

As a child, I was taught, indoctrinated, and inculcated with the idea that I was born inferior by a biased educational system, a prejudicial political and legal system, a Caucasian-oriented media industry, and a hypocritical and racist religious system. Since I was inherently a little lower than Caucasian people, I was to accept the way things were and appreciate the few privileges and the rights I did have.

Many of my schoolteachers were themselves what we called "color struck" (they favored fair complexioned black African-American students over the dark-skinned students).

When I complained about racism and segregation, they told me, "Just accept and adjust". I was always a little "different" than the average young rural African-American male from the South. I just could not "accept and adjust" to the way things were without feeling angry or making some type of protest.

I thank God I wasn't in a large city where there was a strong influence from black militants. Given my attitude of anger and bitterness, I would have been easily drawn into one of the violent hate groups such as the Black Muslims or Black Panthers. I expressed my disgust and anger through poetry and other literature. Little did I know that even then, the Holy Spirit was preparing me for salvation and the writing of this book and others to serve as instruments of healing.

This book is based more upon experience and inspiration than on academic research or study, although a great deal of study has gone into the preparation of this work. This is the hour when God is not only requiring, but demanding that the Church address and attack the disease of racism that has caused schism and stagnation in the Body of Christ. Too much is at stake for the Christian leaders and laypersons to ignore the situation. The crisis warrants an all-out and unified effort to eliminate this spiritual cancer, by embracing and internalizing our new life in Christ.

Brethren are despising brethren, churches are hostile to other churches, and Christians treat one another like enemies – all because of racism. Anyone who reads this book in light of the Gospel with an open mind and considers what the Holy Spirit has inspired me to write concerning racism will be released completely from the bondage of bigotry.

There are 11 chapters in this book, and it is my conviction that this is not coincidental, but an act of providence. Eleven is the number for judgment. Divine justice has issued its final verdict to all perpetrators who continue to allow the devil to continue to blind them and give them an evil heart of racism. Either we will judge ourselves in this area and renounce racism, or God will judge us Himself. The Church has come a long way. There is yet more ground to cover. It is not God's desire that any man should perish, but that all would come to repentance. The Bride of Christ must be without the blemish or spots of racism. May we step up and embrace our newness of life that enables us to love all of God's creation.

For if we would judge ourselves, we should not be judged. But when we are judged, we are chastened of the Lord, that we should not be condemned with the world (1st Corinthians 11:31-32).

Oral Roberts declared, "Racism is perhaps one of the most stubborn problems in the American church, with deep historical roots and a variety of subtle expressions."[1] Billy Graham was once asked on a national televised interview, "If you could change any one thing, what would it be?" His answer was racism!

With this in view, we shall proceed to unmask and expose the real deceptive forces behind racism in the Church. Our true objective is to see Jesus Christ seated on the throne of each Christian's heart and in the place of preeminence in every local church. When this is finally realized, the darkness and degeneracy of racism in the Church will be no more.

Chapter One
Are We Salt And Light?

Ye are the salt of the earth: but if the salt have lost his savour, wherewith shall it be salted? it is thenceforth good for nothing, but to be cast out, and to be trodden under foot of men. Ye are the light of the world. A city that is set on an hill cannot be hid. Neither do men light a candle, and put it under a bushel, but on a candlestick; and it giveth light unto all that are in the house. Let your light so shine before men, that they may see your good works, and glorify your Father which is in heaven (Matthew 5:13-16).

I once watched a documentary about racism on an educational channel, and I left that program feeling angry and grieved in my spirit. I was not irritated or saddened by the racial attitudes of the people who were chosen and secretly filmed for the documentary (whether they were African-American or Caucasian). I was angry over the fact that military organizations have emerged as the most aggressive and effective opponents of racism in institutional America. This alarmed and disturbed me because the church should have taken the leading role in this area.

The redeemed are supposed to set the trends for righteousness and morality – not military organizations or corporate America. We should not be taking a back seat to the academic community or even the political sector in the area of equality and personal freedoms! Jesus Christ described His Church as "the salt of the earth and light of the world". The Creator of language carefully chose those terms when describing His Church for at least two important reasons: to instruct us in the way of holiness, and to obligate us to take the lead in opposing every form of degeneracy and darkness.

Before the invention of refrigerators, salt was used extensively as a food preservative because it effectively delays the natural decaying process. In the same way, the Church is the salt, or preservative, of the earth. It is our responsibility to delay, constrain, and withhold (to hold down or fast) the influence of evil in this world according to Paul in 2nd Thessalonians 2:6. We are the light of the world and children of the day, not of the night. John said, *"In Him was life, and the life was the light of men. And the light shineth in darkness; and the darkness comprehended it not"* (John 1:4-5).

Again, a new commandment I write unto you, which thing is true in him and in you: because the darkness is past, and the true light now shineth. He that saith he is in the light, and hateth his brother, is in darkness even until now. He that loveth his brother abideth in the light, and there is none occasion of stumbling in him.

But he that hateth his brother is in darkness, and walketh in darkness, and knoweth not whither he goeth, because that darkness hath blinded his eyes (1st John 2:8-11).

John Gimenez wrote in his book, **God the Boxer**, "As the Church goes, so goes the world."[2] This is a very true statement. Martin Luther King, Jr., once said, "It is appalling that the most segregated hour of Christian America is 11 o'clock on Sunday morning, the same hour when many are standing to sing, 'In Christ There Is No East Nor West'."[3] The irony of this is not what is practiced, but where it is practiced. It is an insult to God and a shame upon the Church that we have allowed this blight to remain unchallenged and dominant in the Body of Christ!

If the military, political, and academic sectors can confront and challenge the demons of racism and discrimination with some degree of effectiveness, the Church should be able to completely conquer and consume it in the love of God! We have the ability! We have the capability! We have unlimited spiritual resources to not only deal with the consequences of racism, but to also uproot and remove its very causes. The only things we lack are resolve and obedience.

Are we determined enough to obey God, regardless of how we feel, what we were taught, or what others might say about racism? Are you bold enough to deviate from the norm? Are you willing to be "peculiar", to separate yourself from the crowd and join the obedient minority in the Body of Christ that is willing to confront, challenge, and conquer racism in the Church? This is the day of battle. God is going to inspire and energize you for greater service in love.

This is the hour to "beat your plowshares into swords and your pruninghooks into spears…" (Joel 3:10), to fight the good fight of faith against seemingly impossible odds.

Like Gideon's gallant 300 (see Judges 7:7), we are few in number but strong in faith. It is ordained that we prevail over the "Midianites" of racism because the Lord is on our side. We are the salt of the earth and the light of the world, and no evil can defeat us. The Greater One is in us, among us, and before us. He is our Banner. Although the wall of racism seems indestructible and impenetrable, like the walls of Jericho, it too shall crumble at our feet.

I believe that the Church as a whole is about to experience a revival that will melt many hardened hearts and uproot the racism and bigotry that binds them. Bible prophecy demands it. According to the apostle Paul, the Church cannot be perfected and truly unified without this (see Ephesians 4:11-16)! The question you and I have to ask is this: "Will I accept the inevitable and become the salt and light of this new unstoppable wave of the Holy Spirit – or will I continue to live in the flesh, in open opposition to the divine decree to renounce and abolish racism in the Church?"

The Stone that humanistic and religious builders rejected awaits your answer. He is listening for your reply that he might respond.

Jesus saith unto them, Did ye never read in the scriptures, The stone which the builders rejected, the same is become the head of the corner: this is the Lord's doing, and it is marvellous in our eyes?

Therefore say I unto you, The kingdom of God shall be taken from you, and given to a nation bringing forth the fruits thereof. And whosoever shall fall on this stone shall be broken: but on whomsoever it shall fall, it will grind him to powder (Matthew 21:42-44).

CHAPTER TWO
Defining The Disease of Racism

We can't begin to remove racism until we have accurately defined it. We need to understand exactly what we are dealing with before we go to war. The American Heritage Dictionary simply and concisely defines racism as "the notion that one's own ethnic stock is superior." The brief definition gives us a common foundation upon which to begin our examination of racism.

Racism is the mother of bigotry, discrimination, "Jim Crowism" (discrimination against African-Americans by 'legal" means or sanctions), and Nazism, the "white supremacy" movement. All of these belief systems and ideologies spring from an attitude of superiority over others who are different. Adolph Hitler used the preposterous ideas of Aryan superiority trumpeted in his book, Mein Kampf, to mesmerize and mobilize the populace of Germany and launch the misery of World War II. This same evil and deep- rooted belief is still ingrained in the minds of many Caucasians in America and South Africa today, respectively perpetuating discrimination and apartheid in these nations.

Racism is the dragon manipulating such hate groups as the Neo-Nazis, the skinheads, the Ku Klux Klan (KKK), the Black Muslims, and any other sect that promotes racism --- regardless of their ethnicity. Racism seems to come in three forms according to its source.

Hereditary Racism

O Lord, my strength, and my fortress, and my refuge in the day of affliction, the Gentiles shall come unto thee from the ends of the earth, and shall say, Surely our fathers have inherited lies, vanity, and things wherein there is no profit (Jeremiah 16:19).

The word of the Lord came unto me again, saying, What mean ye, that ye use this proverb concerning the land of Israel, saying, The fathers have eaten sour grapes, and the children's teeth are set on edge? (Ezekiel 18:1-2)

These two Bible passages describe the pain of hereditary racism, born of racial attitudes, beliefs, and false concepts of ethnic superiority passed down from parent to child, from one generation to the next. This is the most common way that the disease of racism breeds and continues to thrive in the Church. Like sickle-cell anemia and other hereditary diseases, racism may be transmitted from parents to child at conception through a generational spirit, which often goes undetected.

This spirit's assignment is to make the child become just like its parents in regard to racism. This might sound a little far-fetched to some, but it is a proven fact that the attitudes of mothers during various trimester periods of pregnancy have significant emotional, psychological, and physical effects on their children.

Even worse are the racial concepts and beliefs a child often assimilates from parents during the first five years of life. This is the most critical and active period of learning and mental growth in any person's life. Any seeds of racism planted in this period remain buried in the heart until the child confronts a situation that activates the disease. Many Caucasian people in America and in the Church, who are or were racist, fall in this category. They inherited the lie of racism, and naturally adopted the attitude of ethnic superiority modeled and continually reinforced by their parents and ancestors.

This does not justify or excuse African-Americans and other minorities who also fall into this racist category. Unfortunately, a growing number of African-Americans and other ethnic groups within Christendom may be classified in this group because they are actively teaching their children to be racist under the guise of religious instruction.

Environmental Racism

He that walketh with wise men shall be wise: but a companion of fools shall be destroyed (Proverbs 13:20).

Woe unto you, scribes and Pharisees, hypocrites! for ye compass sea and land to make one proselyte, and when he is made, ye make him twofold more the child of hell than yourselves (Matthew 23:15).

Be not deceived: evil communications corrupt good manners (1st Corinthians 15:33).

Environmental Racism consists of the racial attitudes, beliefs, and erroneous concepts of ethnic superiority caused by the overpowering influence of one's environment and association. People who join or align themselves with hate groups and racist organizations such as the KKK, skinheads, neo-Nazis, the Black Muslims, and even certain exclusive religious denominations (the Mormons have been accused of falling into this category, even though they have recently tried to conceal their racial policies and teachings) are prime examples and victims of environmental racism.

The first Caucasian family to join our predominantly African-American congregation had a son whom I will call Ron. He was enticed into a racist group through pressures exerted by the racist environment that pervaded our southern city. Being a New Englander and having belonged to an integrated church in the northern state, Ron had no problems fitting in with our youth when his family joined the church. As time passed, however, he was drawn into the "southern white mind-set" because of his gullibility and poor selection of friends.

I began to detect a change of attitude and character in this once likable and unbiased young man from New England. You can tell when people are struggling with a superiority attitude stimulated by racism. Ron began to find it difficult to speak to me or greet me in public, and he did everything within his power to avoid me. When he attended church with his parents, he started to feel out of place and complain. Finally, he stopped coming to church, and his parents allowed him to attend another church with some of his Caucasian friends. He soon became completely rebellious toward the Christian life style and toward his parents. At the time of this writing, Ron is being held back as a senior in high school, and is forced to take remedial course to graduate. He had lost his focus on God along with his sense of purpose and destiny.

What happened to Ron is a classic example of what environmental racism can do to a person. It can blind a person's mind to reality and the real issues of life. Its victims begin to resent and even hate the very people they once loved simply because they look, sound, or believe differently from them. This brand of racism strikes every race and color. Many African-Americans are being enticed and converted to the racist ideology of black supremacy groups such as "Nation of Islam".

No one is completely immune to catching the virus of racism – regardless of their race – if they insist upon walking in the counsel of ungodly people who promote bigotry and hatred.

Blessed is the man that walketh not in the counsel of the ungodly, nor standeth in the way of sinners, nor sitteth in the seat of the scornful (Psalm 1:1).

Make no friendship with an angry man; and with a furious man thou shalt not go: Lest thou learn his ways, and get a snare to thy soul (Proverbs 22:24-25)

Reactionary/Reverse Racism

And if a man cause a blemish in his neighbour; as he hath done, so shall it be done to him; breach for breach, eye for eye, tooth for tooth: as he hath caused a blemish in a man, so shall it be done to him again (Leviticus 24:19-20).

Reactionary/reverse racism is rooted in the extreme application of this obsolete Levitical law on a personal level. In its racist form, this way of thinking is humanistic and downright devilish. Reactionary/reverse racism consists of the racial attitudes, beliefs, and erroneous concepts of ethnic superiority triggered in a suppressed minority by ill treatment and acts of racism inflicted by members of other dominant groups. At one time, I was a proponent of this insane belief (more will be said about this later on), and I speak from experience on this issue. In my experience, I have found that the average African-American in or out of the Church is not overtly racist. Those who are tend to fall into this group.

Most African-Americans are not taught from birth that they are superior to any other ethnic group because of their color. The exceptions tend to be children with parents who belong to groups that actively promote racism and race separation. In general, the opposite extreme is our problem. We battle an ethnic inferiority complex developed over several hundred years of dehumanizing slavery, subsequent racism, segregation, and discrimination. As a result, most African-Americans face a formidable battle to find equality in their own minds – a fight many lose before they ever reach the marketplace or job site.

However, there is an alarming rise in reactionary/reverse racism among young African-Americans that is frightening. There is only one answer and antidote to this raging fire fueled by people like Louis Farrakhan, the successor to the late Elijah Muhammad, founder of the "Nation of Islam". That answer is the gospel of Christ and the Church.

We must take a unified stand against all racism, regardless of what category it falls under. We must love our neighbors as ourselves, regardless of their color, but this requires us to be strong enough in the Lord to turn the other cheek if we are rejected, slurred, or slandered. As Christians, you and I must put the teachings of the Bible before all other beliefs, concepts, or human traditions, whether we are black or white, red or yellow. God hates racism in any form, regardless of how we classify it or try to justify it by twisting Scripture and listing the wrongs we've endured. Racism is sin in His sight!

CHAPTER THREE
The Roots of Racism

Like other malignant diseases, the disease of racism springs up from a root, or can be traced to a cause. If we ever expect to completely conquer it, we must first identify racisms roots. I have been able to isolate several root causes of racism, and each one in itself is part of a root system that gives life and strength to this deadly disease.

Degeneracy

Behold, I was shapen in iniquity; and in sin did my mother conceive me (Psalm 51:5).

The very taproot of racism may well be found in man's innate degenerate nature, implanted in all of us at conception. Although our natures have changed because of our spiritual regeneration through Jesus, our unregenerate flesh still retains a great degree of the old Adamic nature. All sin (and racism is a sin) stems from our carnal nature and natural appetites. Our degenerate human nature must be "mortified" or put to death and brought under subjection. Human degeneracy is not the sin of racism, but it is the "soil" from which the seed sprouts in the human soul. Christians who have a problem with racism can find wise counsel in the words of Jeremiah the prophet:

For thus saith the Lord to the men of Judah and Jerusalem, Break up your fallow ground, and sow not among thorns. Circumcise yourselves to the Lord, and take away the foreskins of your heart, ye men of Judah and inhabitants of Jerusalem: lest my fury come forth like fire, and burn that none can quench it, because of the evil of your doings (Jeremiah 4:3-4).

Pride

Pride goeth before destruction, and an haughty spirit before a fall (Proverbs 16:18).

Pride is one of the most prolific roots of racism. There are four different branches or types of pride we must guard against. They include the pride of place, face, grace, and race.

The "pride of place" deals with a person's pride over his status or position in life. The "pride of face" concerns an individual's pride about the ability to maintain an image that is superior to other people. It is usually related to some physical or visual attribute inherited at birth. The term, "beautiful people", as it applies to movie starts, glamor models, and socialites, perfectly describes one of the aspects of this type of pride. "Pride of grace" describes religious or denominational pride.

The "pride of race" deals with pride based on skin color or ethnicity. Segregation is perhaps more evident in the Church than in any other American institution, and race pride is the most likely reason for the problem. Many born-again and Spirit-filled believers have difficulty looking beyond skin color and ethnicity. Their ability to see people through the eyes of God (from the inside out) has been blurred and distorted by the cataracts of bigotry, ignorance, and fear. Though race pride is present in every ethnic group represented in the body of Christ, it appears to be most prevalent in the attitudes displayed by many Caucasians believers toward their African-American counterparts. There are exceptions to this pattern, of course, but we have a long way to go to overcome or mortify race pride in the Church.

Personally, I have noticed that the average African-American Christian seems to have no problem fellowshipping with Caucasian brethren. The predominantly African-American fellowships I have attended or pastored have always welcomed Caucasians into their services and treated them with great respect and dignity. I believe the most of the "crossing over" and the fellowship has been one-sided.

The African-American churches I have been acquainted with regularly invited Caucasians ministers in to minister on various occasions. In recent years, African-American Christians have begun joining predominantly Caucasian congregations at a somewhat increased rate, when you consider that Caucasian Christians seldom join predominantly African-American congregations (especially if the leadership is African-American).

Superiority Complex

For I say, through the grace given unto me, to every man that is among you, not to think of himself more highly than he ought to think; but to think soberly, according as God hath dealt to every man the measure of faith. (Romans 12:3).

"Superiority complexes" constitute one of the major causes of racism in the Church and society. Although some would call this a psychological term, the fact is that this form of pride is perfectly described in the Book of Romans as "thinking of yourself more highly than you ought to". People with racist beliefs exaggerate their importance and ethnicity to overshadow the value of others who are different from them.

The Jews in Jesus' day believed that they were superior to other races and nations because of their racial ancestry and religious heritage. They were so steeped in their pride and superior attitude that they eventually suffocated their own nation. This affliction is the same plague that has birthed segregation in Christendom. This is the reason that most Caucasianb Christians are reluctant or even refuses to fellowship with predominantly African-American churches (though some will not admit it). This biased mind-set prevents most Caucasian believers who are searching for a church home from even considering attendance at a predominantly African-American church.

A prominent Caucasian couple in our town visited our church once. This seemingly sincere Christian couple was captivated and deeply impressed by our order of service and the presence of the Lord that filled and glorified the house. The husband was so moved by what he saw and experienced that he said, "This is one of the most spiritual churches that

I have ever been in, and it is the most spiritual church that I have visited in South Carolina".

As a leader in the Gideons International, he had visited many churches in and out of the state (both African-Americans and Caucasian). The irony of this story is that I later discovered that the couple was actively looking for a new church home. If this man's statement expressed his sincere and genuine estimation of our predominantly African-American congregation, why wouldn't he and his wife consider joining "the most spiritual church he had visited" in the state?

Our church is located in a region that has embraced race segregation since the founding of the nation. Even today, the pressure of the status quo makes it difficult for people to cross the "race line" in any area of life. For this reason, people like the couple who visited our church are rarely able to overcome the pressures of ingrained racial pride and superiority.

I do not mean to sound hard, but if racism in the Church is to ever be conquered, Caucasian believers (who constitute the vast majority of believers in the American population of the Church) need to realistically evaluate their attitudes about their African-American brethren and those of other minority groups. This superiority complex must be exposed and destroyed so that equality will abound and unity will be achieved.

Ignorance

My people are destroyed for lack of knowledge: because thou hast rejected knowledge, I will also reject

> *thee, that thou shalt be no priest to me: seeing thou hast forgotten the law of thy God, I will also forget thy children* (Hosea 4:6).
>
> *Then said Jesus to those Jews which believed on him, If ye continue in my word, then are ye my disciples indeed; And ye shall know the truth, and the truth shall make you free* (John 8:31-32).

I believe that ignorance is one of the major causes of racism. Racism and every other evil that lurks in the degeneracy of man's dark side thrives on ignorance! Ignorance is "the absence of knowledge, wisdom, or understanding."

Ignorance has fostered many absurd concepts and doctrines of devils in the intellect of countless narrow-minded men who professed to be wise. Many racist groups, such as the Mormons, the black Muslims, the skinheads, and others, are often formed on the wild, fiercely defended views of isolated men who, like their followers, are marooned on the "Island of Ignorance and Idiocy."

I am sad to say that many Christians of various ethnic backgrounds are also shipwrecked and stranded on this same island due to their racist ways. Why? They have either rejected God's knowledge for the wisdom of man (see Jeremiah 8:9), or they have failed to study God's Word for enlightenment and emancipation in the area of racism.

What is the answer to this sad and shameful situation in Christendom? Racism causes Christian brethren to be hateful, hostile, and harmful to one another simply because their skin color and ethnic roots are different. The believers in the first century church overcame racism.

Preachers and church leaders today must also be bold and informed enough to preach and teach the truth about racism and eliminate it from the Body! They must cry aloud and spare not. They should not be timid or intimidated by those in their flocks who voice opposing views or exert prominent influence.

The Lord will justify and uphold any leader who dares to speak the truth in love! The Holy Spirit has already gone before any pastor who will have faith enough to follow the Lord's lead and feed the flock with knowledge and understanding concerning the issue of racism. The fallow ground of many hearts have already been broken and convicted; they only await the seed of confirmation from the sower!

Fear

The fear of man bringeth a snare: but whoso putteth his trust in the Lord shall be safe (Proverbs 29:25).

For God hath not given us the spirit of fear; but of power, and of love, and of a sound mind (2nd Timothy 1:7).

If ignorance is a root of racism, then fear is its offspring! Many Christians continue to embrace their racist precepts, policies, and practices only because of fear.
They fear what they don't know. They are afraid to fellowship with people who are not of their race because they fear what it might produce in other areas.

Many people simple fear change. If they knew God's Word, they would know that the fear of man leads to a snare and that God did not give them a spirit of fear (see Proverbs 29:25; 2nd Timothy 1:7). Fear that is conceived in ignorance also thrives on complacency. Too many Christians live in the comfort zone of complacency, and they carefully avoid facing the reality of racial issues because of fear.

They are too afraid to venture out beyond their narrow-minded concepts to create friendships, fellowships, and relationships with people who are not their color.

Fear isolates and separates believers of one race from believers of other races who share common beliefs and commitments. These believers know in their hearts that the racist precepts, policies, and practices of their local churches are unscriptural and wrong. However, they are too afraid and timid to challenge "Goliath," so they flow with the crowd. The Word of God holds the key to their release from bondage, and it will expose them to a whole new realm of faith and obedience:

> *I sought the Lord, and he heard me, and delivered me from all my fears (Psalm 34:4).*

> *There is no fear in love; but perfect love casteth out fear: because fear hath torment. He that feareth is not made perfect in love (1st John 4:18).*

Prayer and love open the door of deliverance from racism. Just as the Psalmist sought God and was delivered from all his fears, any Christian who feels paralyzed and unable to stand against the evils of racism must pray for deliverance.

Prayer, coupled with the perfect love of Christ in our hearts, will remove fear and its paralyzing effect on our ability to confront, challenge, and conquer racism.

We have considered five of the most common causes of racism in the Church, but there are many others we could have discussed.

However, the central issue is this: What are you going to do about the things that breed racism in your life?

Will you continue to allow this virus to enter uncontested, or will you do something about those things? Don't think that the enemy is going to be satisfied until he completely destroys you. The truth is that you and I must get rid of this evil disease before it gets rid of us!

CHAPTER FOUR
The Reality of Racism in the Church

It is of no use to hide from the truth when God is determined to expose it; Racism is a reality in the Church! God's people have battled with prejudice and racism since the time of Noah! Many people (especially African-Americans) will be surprised to learn that racism did not originate with Caucasian men.

Racism in the Old Testament

Now these are the generations of the sons of Noah, Shem, Ham, and Japheth: and unto them were sons born after the flood...And the sons of Ham; Cush, and Mizraim, and Phut, and Canaan (Genesis 10:1, 6).

Racism began with the division of the human race through the three sons of Noah after the Great Flood. Anthropology lists many diverse races, but according to the Bible, every modern race of man is descended from the three sons of Noah:
1. Shemites *(Hebrews, Arabs, and others)*
2. Japhetites *(Caucasians)*

3. Hamites *(Negroes, Canaanites, Egyptians, Libyans, Mongolians)*

The "table of nations" (found in Genesis 10:1-32) implies that Hamites (the descendants of Ham, Noah's youngest son) were the first prominent or dominant race. These descendants of Noah's black son, Ham (the word means "dark or swarthy") rose to prominence at this early stage of civilization. Many scholars, historians, and theologians are convinced that Nimrod, the grandson of Ham and the son of Cush, who was called the first "mighty one" after the flood, also introduced racism and slavery in the earth!

And Cush begat Nimrod: he began to be a mighty one in the earth. He was a mighty hunter before the Lord: wherefore it is said, Even as Nimrod the mighty hunter before the Lord. And the beginning of his kingdom was Babel, and Erech, and Accad, and Calneh, in the land of Shinar (Genesis 10:8-10).

Nimrod appears to have been a despot who felt himself superior to all other men. He was a hunter and enslaver of men, and was perhaps the first world ruler. Babel or Babylon, the site of the "Tower of Babel", was the beginning of his kingdom. It is logical to conclude that the majority of the ruling Hamitic (black) race was conspirators with their favorite son, Nimrod. As a African-American man, that is a bitter pill to swallow. However, as a minister and writer, I must proclaim and publish things from a true biblical perspective. So as bad as it seems to this African-American who is now a part of a minority group being victimized by racism, I have to accept the fact that my ancestors probably started the wheel of racism rolling!

Each of the three distinct racial groups had their day as the dominant ruling race on the earth, and each has failed miserably. The descendants of Japheth currently dominate the world. Each of the dominant races perpetuated the racism their predecessors practiced. I thank God that a new race is emerging in the human family—the race of the redeemed. This holy race is destined to break the vicious cycle and reign in righteousness with the King of kings throughout eternity!

Racism In Egypt

Now there arose up a new king over Egypt, which knew not Joseph. And he said unto his people, Behold, the people of the children of Israel are more and mightier than we: Come on, let us deal wisely with them; lest they multiply, and it come to pass, that, when there falleth out any war, they join also unto our enemies, and fight against us, and so get them up out of the land. Therefore they did set over them taskmasters to afflict them with their burdens. And they built for Pharaoh treasure cities, Pithom and Raamses. But the more they afflicted them, the more they multiplied and grew. And they were grieved because of the children of Israel. And the Egyptians made the children of Israel to serve with rigour:

And they made their lives bitter with hard bondage, in morter, and in brick, and in all manner of service in the field: all their service, wherein they made them serve, was with rigour (Exodus 1:8-14).

The Psalmist called Egypt *"the land of Ham"* (see Psalm 105:23-27). According to the first chapter of the Book of Exodus, the *"land of Ham"* was the first nation to enslave an entire ethnic group. Apart from providence and fear, it was sheer racism that motivated the Egyptians, who were descendants of Ham and the present world rulers at that time, kept the wheel of racism rolling.

Racism in the Church in the Wilderness

This is that Moses, which said unto the children of Israel, A prophet shall the Lord your God raise up unto you of your brethren, like unto me; him shall ye hear. This is he, that was in the church in the wilderness with the angel which spake to him in the mount Sina, and with our fathers: who received the lively oracles to give unto us (Acts 7:37-38).

And Miriam and Aaron spake against Moses because of the Ethiopian woman whom he had married: for he had married an Ethiopian woman. And they said, Hath the Lord indeed spoken only by Moses? hath he not spoken also by us? And the Lord heard it (Numbers 12:1-2).

Why were Miriam and Aaron so adamantly opposed to Moses' marriage to Zipporah, the daughter of Jethro?

And the Lord spake suddenly unto Moses, and unto Aaron, and unto Miriam, Come out ye three unto the tabernacle of the congregation. And they three came out.

> *With him will I speak mouth to mouth, even apparently, and not in dark speeches; and the similitude of the Lord shall he behold: wherefore then were ye not afraid to speak against my servant Moses? And the anger of the Lord was kindled against them; and he departed (Numbers 12:4,8-9).*

God was angry with Miriam and Aaron because of their attitude and their open opposition to Moses. Why? God saw that the real motives behind their attitudes and opposition were jealousy and racism, in that order. They envied Moses, and they tried to use the fact that he had married an Ethiopian (Cushitic) woman against him. God's swift and decisive judgment of their jealousy and racism should serve as a warning to the church today. The same God, who opposed racism in the Church in the wilderness, is also opposed to racism in the Church today!

Racism In the New Testament

> *Then saith the woman of Samaria unto him, How is it that thou, being a Jew, askest drink of me, which am a woman of Samaria? for the Jews have no dealings with the Samaritans (John 4:9). And he said unto them, Ye know how that it is an unlawful thing for a man that is a Jew to keep company, or come unto one of another nation; but God hath shewed me that I should not call any man common or unclean (Acts 10:28).*

Jewish people in Jesus' day and in the post-resurrection era possessed a superiority complex. Their pride in their ethnic and religious heritage made them so out of touch with God that they actually thought they were superior to all other people on the face of the earth. The descendants of Abraham were chosen by God to become a nation through which He would send His Son, the prophets, and the written Word. They became blinded by their own inflated ideas of self-worth. This racial superiority complex was so prominent and persuasive in Israel that traces of it even permeated the early Church!

Paul had to publicly confront Peter about his spirit of superiority and racism:

> *But when Peter was come to Antioch, I withstood him to the face, because he was to be blamed. For before that certain came from James, he did eat with the Gentiles: but when they were come, he withdrew and separated himself, fearing them which were of the circumcision* (Galatians 2:11-12).

Early American Racism

On Sunday morning in November of 1786, a little band of African-American Christians arrived at the front door of St. George's Methodist Episcopal Church in Philadelphia. When the sexton pointed to the gallery, the blacks paused briefly and then started up the rickety stairs with downcast eyes and heavy hearts. To the leaders of this group, Richard Allen and Absalom Jones, this was the ultimate indignity—to be shunted from the first floor, where there were plenty of seats, to the gallery. Free African-American men had helped to build that church!

The group had barely reached the top of the stairs when a voice from the pulpit said, "Let us pray." Without thinking, the men reverently plopped down where they were – in the front of the gallery. Allen was praying as hard as he could when he heard loud voices. He opened his eyes and saw a Caucasian sexton trying to pull Absalom Jones from his knees.

"You must get up; you must not kneel down here!" the sexton said. "Wait until the prayer is over," Jones replied. The voices echoed through the church, and the people looked up to behold the incredible scene of a African-American Christian and a Caucasian Christian wrestling in the house of the Lord! "Get up!" the sexton said. Jones replied wearily, "Wait until the prayer is over, and I will not trouble you any more." Four or five Caucasian church members rushed to the sexton's aid, and the struggle quickly spread over the gallery.

Before the issue was resolved, the prayer ended. The African-American brethren promptly stood up and, without a word, streamed out of the church in the first mass demonstration against religious racism in African-American history. Richard Allen added the mournful postscript: "… And they were no more plagued by us in the church."[5]

This incident marked the beginning of a series of racist incidents in early America that trickled down through the history of the Church in America. If the Church in America would have unified and clearly denounced slavery from this nation's inception, perhaps the slave trade would have dissolved, the Civil War would have been averted, and there would be little, if any, racism or discrimination in America today!

Antebellum Racism in the Church

One of the most significant acts affirming racism in the American Church took place just before the Civil War. The Southern Baptist Convention, reportedly the largest Protestant denomination in America today (numbering approximately 15.6 million members), was formed when Baptists met in Augusta, Georgia, in 1845. The delegates met to debate whether slave owners could become missionaries. In a split that literally foreshadowed the Civil War, the Northern delegates said, "no", so the Southern group broke off into their own denomination.

Sadly, America's largest Protestant denomination, the Southern Baptist Convention, was born of schism and racism that day. What might have taken place if those Southern Christians would have agreed with Scripture and concurred with their Northern brethren on the evils of slavery? Perhaps the Civil War, which claimed millions of American lives on both sides (Union and Confederate), could have been averted!

Contemporary Racism in the Church

Racism is a reality in the church today, although many are either too blind to see it, or too narrow-minded to accept its existence. There are many different types and degrees of racism in the Church, but they must all be exposed and eliminated. There has been some progress. There have been some commendable moved toward integration by the United Methodist Church, The Church of God, The Assemblies of God, and certain Presbyterian synods.

However, in the South where I live, the momentum to integrate among these groups has all but stalled.

Most American churches acknowledge the need to change and correct racial inequities, but they lack the impetus and resolve to actually do it. Unfortunately, there is still a tight nucleus of people in nearly every denomination and group that continues to promote racism based on the idiotic belief that God "does not want the mixing".

The teaching stems from the centuries old phobic myth created by segregationists who claimed they wanted to "protect and preserve the dignity of Caucasian women from the sexual prowess and romantic exploits of the African-American male." History and the present-day presence of so many fair-skinned African-American people of mixed blood prove that the opposite was true. Most interracial relations took place between male Caucasian slave-owners and African-American female slaves (usually without the woman's consent).

Much has changed for the better, but many of the old attitudes and taboos about segregation in the Church remain intact and unchallenged. A good friend of mine, a dear Caucasian brother who is deeply committed to raising money for mission work in Russia, came to our church to solicit money for that purpose. He made his plea, but our people did not respond well financially because they were already obligated to mission work in Africa. He left disappointed because he failed to realize that at the time, there was a greater need in Africa than in Russia, because Russia was already receiving the bulk of American Christian missionary and material support due to high-profile media attention. We were made to feel that our prayerful placement of missionary funds toward Africa was wrong and misplaced!

Racism also surfaces in the discriminatory practices of Christian bankers, businessmen, and employers who endorse policies, procedures, and practices that are based on skin color and ethnicity rather than character, competency, and integrity.

Some time ago, I was invited to minister at a convention in North Carolina. I observed that although about 80% of the congregation was African-American, all of the leadership and the majority of the guest speakers were Caucasians (I was the only African-American speaker). To make matters worse, before the meeting, I was escorted to a waiting room where the senior bishop introduces me to the head officials of the church organization as "Prophet Goings." Immediately, I sensed that some of the brethren present had released a spirit of racism and intimidation toward me. I could almost hear them say in their hearts, "How dare you! How could you allow yourself, a African-American,' to be called a prophet?" The senior bishop had already been introduced to the prophetic ministry and the mantle under which I flow. He was fully confident that I would live up to his billing.

To further aggravate the situation, when I passed out a few of my books to these would-be writers (who had not published any books yet), I unknowingly added injury to insult in their minds. The fact that I was a "published author" seemed to completely offend their egos and sense of racial superiority. One brother in particular seemed to turn bright red every time it was revealed that I had achieved some success in certain areas where he had not. Finally, he could no longer stand to be upstaged by a African-American (even though I was the keynote speaker), and he abruptly left the room.

Although I had ministered in national conventions, crusades, and revivals before as an evangelist, this was my first encounter of this kind of intimidation and racism. I am thankful that the Lord—apart from any conscious effort on my part—completely confounded and devastated my racist critics that night by the revelation and confirmation of the Word through the manifestation of the Spirit.

This subtle type of racism is directed by many Caucasian clergymen and laymen toward African-American ministers. This racial superiority complex has been passed down through generations of racism, and in many cases, these sincere brethren don't even realize it is there! They unconsciously or consciously presume that African-American ministers, as a whole, are not competent or intelligent enough to teach or lead them. Perhaps this is why many traditional Pentecostal and Charismatic groups are reluctant to acknowledge and honor William Seymour as a foundational father of the Pentecostal movement.

Racism in the Church will never be eliminated unless her leaders take a unified and uncompromising stand against it.

They must be bold enough to stand on the Word; regardless of what sentiments their congregations or communities hold in the area of racial issues. I respect and appreciate men like Oral Roberts, Kelly Varner, John Mears, and others who have stepped to the front line in the battle to break down racial walls in the Church.

They openly acknowledge the existence of racial bias, and they have openly and boldly spoken out against the sin of racial prejudice. I am convinced that the answer to the stubborn racial problem plaguing the Church today will be found in the pulpit, not in the pews. Leadership in righteousness comes from the clergy and not the laity.

CHAPTER FIVE
5 The Consequence and Detriment of Racism in Christendom

Ye are the salt of the earth: but if the salt have lost his savour, wherewith shall it be salted? it is thenceforth good for nothing, but to be cast out, and to be trodden under foot of men. Ye are the light of the world. A city that is set on an hill cannot be hid. Neither do men light a candle, and put it under a bushel, but on a candlestick; and it giveth light unto all that are in the house. Let your light so shine before men, that they may see your good works, and glorify your Father which is in heaven (Matthew 5:13-16).

Jesus made it clear that Christians are the salt of the earth and the light of the world. What are the consequences if the Church does not address and attack the cancer of racism among its own members? What consequences and detriment have we already suffered because of the racist attitudes held by past generations of believers? Again, I refer to these principled words of John Gimenez, "As the Church goes, so goes the world."

Slavery In America

The inhuman and brutal slave trade in America lasted for well over 200 years, taking the lives of multiple millions of Africans in the process. All of this brutality, pain, and needless death could have been avoided if the Church of that day would have taken a unified stand against slavery. Unfortunately, history proves that the contrary took place!

Many of the people involved in the exportation and exploitation of Africans were established members of the Church. Some even tried to "justify" slavery by twisting the Word of God to defend their cruel practices. These efforts birthed such ridiculous beliefs as Africans being "subhuman and specially suited for servitude." Erroneous teachings like the "curse of Ham" (we will deal with this topic in the next chapter) became a favorite lesson of bigots.

Others tried to justify racism and slavery by declaring that Negroes were heathenish, and therefore, they were "better off" as slaves in America than as free men in Africa. These ideas were merely racial bias dressed in religion, predicated solely on racism and a racial superiority complex. It is absurd to think that "heathenism" (aren't we all "heathen" until we repent and receive Jesus Christ as Lord?) or any other ungodly or humanistic belief system held by one group justifies their enslavement and exploitation by another "saved" group.

The Bible clearly reveals that all Gentile nations (regardless of race) were aliens from the truth and separated from God (see Ephesians 2:11-12). So in the light of the Word of God, racism and materialism were the true motivations behind slavery in America.

Had the Church made a stand against racism and blown the trumpet, as it should have, slavery in America would have died in its infancy.

Segregation in America

The highly profitable and publicly accepted institution of slavery birthed the unconstitutional, unfair an unjust system of segregation—even in the Church. Jesus said, *"Every kingdom divided against itself is brought to desolation; and every city or house divided against itself shall not stand"* (Matthew 12:25^b). When the American Church actually practiced and promoted segregation within itself, it set a trend and example for the whole world to follow. Instead of being the salt and light of the world, as it should have, it literally took the lead in promoting and perpetuating segregation!

I claimed earlier that the church is perhaps the most segregated institution in America. This is a shameful indication of the racist heritage that has long been associated with the Church in America. Although there is a glimmer of hope on the horizon concerning the decline and fall of racial barriers in the Body of Christ, far too many Christians are complacent and content with the way things are.

I am convinced that God in His sovereignty will soon shake up the Church in regard to the ethnic walls that divide His people.

God will shake everything that can be shaken to see His Word fulfilled, and to bring believers into unity of the faith (see Hebrews 12:27). Every attitude, concept, and human concoction that opposes and exalts itself against the will of

God will be pulled down either voluntarily by man, or forcibly by the sovereign power of God operating through His servants! (see 2nd Corinthians 10:4-5). Again, if we judge ourselves we will not be judged!

The Holocaust

Some of the ill-informed, brainwashed, and narrow-minded recruits to neo-Nazism, racism, and anti-Semitism loudly claim that the Holocaust, which exterminated millions of Jews during the heyday of Hitler's regime, was a hoax. This racist jargon is utterly insane, but in a way, these people who hold extreme racist attitudes actually wish the Holocaust had never happened! Why? Because the Holocaust publicly exposed the inhuman beast behind racism.

The truth of the matter is that the Holocaust did happen, while the Church as a whole stood on the sidelines of indifference and watched the slaughter! Could the Holocaust have been prevented if the Church would have gotten involved an sounded the trumpet? I cannot answer that question because of the prophetic implications involved. However, I do believe that more lives could have been saved if the Church in Germany and other European nations would have stepped forward in unity against Hitler's program of racism, anti-Semitism, and supposed Aryan supremacy. But then, how could an institution with its own history of racism and segregation "pull the mote" out of the eyes of Adolf Hitler?

The Plight of African-Americans and Other Minorities Today

There is a definite connection between racism in the Church and what is happening in the African-America, Hispanic, and other minority communities. It is a fact that a great percentage of the people at the helm of industry, banking, media, and business as a whole are white males who are also church affiliated! This confirms this assertion. Although we cannot fully blame these leaders, they must shoulder a great degree of the fault because they have the power to do good but don't.

Most minority members of the work force, including African-American and Hispanic workers, are in a dismal and suppressed state because of the racial and discriminatory policies and practices endorsed by church-going business and industry leaders. African-American and other minorities are not given nearly the same consideration, respect, or opportunity as are afforded to their Caucasian counterparts in the job market, the loan office, the real-estate office, and other essential sectors of society.

This "trickle-down" racism stifles the growth of African-American families and communities. When individuals or communities are caged like mice and denied the opportunity to grow and expand, the result is nearly always violence, crime, and chaos. I often wonder if my Christian brethren know that the racial and discriminatory practices they approve or allow have made them accomplices to the systematic destruction of African-American males, families, and communities?

Whenever the topic of the exploitation and ill treatment of African-Americans by Caucasians comes up, the hot subject of "reparation" is also heard. This idea of "repaying" African-Americans for the wrongs endured in previous generations sound good and fair, but the idea is absolutely unfeasible because of the nation's economic plight. However, I believe I speak for the majority of African-Americans and other minorities when I say, "Give me no reparation or hand-outs, just give me the same consideration, equality, and opportunity to obey God that Caucasian Americans have, and I will be all right!"

Constipation, Stagnation, and Racial Schism in the Church

The final detriment racism has brought to the Church is threefold. The first of these three morbid conditions is "spiritual constipation", or the sluggish state of the "spiritual bowels" in which there is no constant flow or release of love, mercy, and the fruit of the Spirit:

> *Put on therefore, as the elect of God, holy and beloved, bowels of mercies, kindness, humbleness of mind, meekness, longsuffering; Forbearing one another, and forgiving one another, if any man have a quarrel against any: even as Christ forgave you, so also do ye. And above all these things put on charity, which is the bond of perfectness (Colossians 3:12-14).*

> *Whosoever hateth his brother is a murderer: and ye know that no murderer hath eternal life abiding in him. Hereby perceive we the love of God, because he laid down his life for us: and we ought to lay down*

our lives for the brethren. But whoso hath this world's good, and seeth his brother have need, and shutteth up his bowels of compassion from him, how dwelleth the love of God in him? (1ˢᵗ John 3:15-17)

These Scriptures make it clear: any Christian who practices racism in the church, on the job, or in any other place is "constipated". If you harbor prejudice or racist thoughts in your heart, the only thing that will break your "bowels" loose is a good dose of the "laxative" of love. When I was growing up, I sometimes found myself constipated for various reasons. My mother would take a small bottle of nasty-tasting castor oil and make me gulp some down. That stuff tasted so bad that it would almost knock me out! However bitter it tasted in my mouth, it would always break my bowels loose and free me of the pain and agony of constipation.

A great segment of the Church needs a dose of spiritual "castor oil". It needs to be freed from spiritual constipation so that their bowels of love can rid them of ethnic supremacy, pride, ignorance, fear, hatred, and any other vain attitude, concept, or emotion associated with racism!

The second morbid sickness racism fostered in the Body is "spiritual stagnation". Spiritual stagnation is the offshoot of spiritual constipation, but it takes the first condition to a more severe and serious level. It is the complete stoppage of the flow of love in our lives. Every first graded knows that when anything is designed to run or flow like a river, and it loses its ability to do so, a buildup of waste, germs, and other foul things begins to collect. This vile blockage begins to form a cesspool.

Racism in the Church has created a cesspool of filth that stinks in the nostrils of God. He condemns it and demands its immediate destruction!

Schism in the Body of Christ is the final result of racism in the Church. The apostle Paul warned about schism in 1st Corinthians 12:24-25. Though many Church schisms (opposing groups in division) stem from such things as denominational division and doctrine, the racial barrier is by far the greatest and most deadly schism because it even divides people of the same denomination and doctrine!

The Church's ability to evangelize the world and restrain the rotten decay of iniquity (which is escalating at an alarming rate) has been compromised and jeopardized by its racist policies and practices. Revival rain has been withheld because of the sin of racism and the division it has created. Unity is a prerequisite to revival, but unity can never be produced or realized in the Body so long as the sin of racism and segregation are condoned and practiced.

Prophecy and prayer demand that these schismatic walls of racism fall! This is why I know God is going to sovereignly intervene and make things right if we do not. The Scriptures, which cannot be broken, demand it. Christ will have a unified and glorified Church at His return.

Each of us should examine ourselves to make sure there is no root of racism in us, no matter what our ethnic roots may be. I am fully convinced that the period of forbearance and winking we have enjoyed in the past is over, for we "who hold the truth in righteousness" (Romans 1:18).

6 CHAPTER SIX
Rightly Dividing the Curse of Ham

And the sons of Noah, that went forth of the ark, were Shem, and Ham, and Japheth: and Ham is the father of Canaan. These are the three sons of Noah: and of them was the whole earth overspread. And Noah began to be an husbandman, and he planted a vineyard: And he drank of the wine, and was drunken; and he was uncovered within his tent. And Ham, the father of Canaan, saw the nakedness of his father, and told his two brethren without. And Shem and Japheth took a garment, and laid it upon both their shoulders, and went backward, and covered the nakedness of their father; and their faces were backward, and they saw not their father's nakedness. And Noah awoke from his wine, and knew what his younger son had done unto him. And he said, Cursed be Canaan; a servant of servants shall he be unto his brethren. And he said, Blessed be the Lord God of Shem; and Canaan shall be his servant. God shall enlarge Japheth, and he shall dwell in the tents of Shem; and Canaan shall be his servant (Genesis 9:18-27).

It would be illogical, if not impossible, to have a serious discussion on racism from a biblical perspective without examining the so-called "curse of Ham". Many Caucasian Christians today (with many from the past), have attempted to justify their belief in racial discrimination and bigotry using the curse Noah pronounced upon one of the sons of Ham and his posterity.

Some years ago, one of my relatives was told by her Caucasian junior high school teacher that people of color were cursed in the bible, and therefore, they were inferior and subservient to Caucasians. The "teacher" cited this particular biblical incident as proof of her racial idiocy. That woman's rash words left a mental scar and sparked anger toward God in my cousin's heart that took years to mend and resolve. This is a classic example of how people have distorted, misinterpreted, and misused the Word of God deceitfully to promote racism and other doctrine of devils.

Study to shew thyself approved unto God, a workman that needeth not to be ashamed, rightly dividing the word of truth (2 Timothy 2:15).

The term, "curse of Ham," is totally inaccurate. Ham was the youngest son of Noah, and his name means "hot or dark, colored or swarthy." His son was named Canaan, and he was the object of the curse—not Ham:

And Noah awoke from his wine, and knew what his younger son had done unto him. And he said, Cursed be Canaan; a servant of servants shall he be unto his brethren (Genesis 9:24-25).

According to the Word of God, the curse of Ham should actually be referred to as "the curse of Canaan". This is an important distinction because many people who are racist just want to lump together all of Ham's descendants under the curse. The black races that descended directly from Ham's son, Cush, are especially cited as being under the so-called "curse of Ham" because we are more Hamitic in appearance than perhaps any of the other ethnic groups in the Hamitic race.

The facts are clear: the curse placed upon Canaan had nothing to do with the rest of Ham descendants! Noah's curse centered exclusively on Canaan's descendants, and that curse was fulfilled from the Semitic perspective when Joshua and the children of Israel conquered and subdued all the Canaanite nations in the Land of Promise!

The descendants of the Japhetic or Caucasian race have unscripturally subjugated people who were not part of the curse of Canaan wrongfully. A great injustice inspired by satan has been committed, and only God can resolve the matter and make the perpetrators that have yielded themselves to this evil pay reparations.

Nevertheless, I believe that every local church (regardless of the race of its members) must rightly divide the Scriptures concerning the so-called "curse of Ham" (Canaan).

It is time to allow the Holy Spirit to bring clarity to this misconstrued issue that has fostered so much racism. It is time for Christians to know the truth about this matter, for the truth alone will make them free.

CHAPTER SEVEN
7 Am I Black or White by Chance or Divine Determination

From time to time, I hear people say, "I am just a Christian who happens to be African-Americans," or I'm a believer who happens to be Caucasian". That sounded like a good statement to me at one time, and I adopted that slogan until the Holy Spirit corrected me. I heard His voice saying in reproof, "Your race and color just did not happen by chance, but by Divine determination."

I began to search out the meaning of "Divine determination," and I discovered that it is similar to predestination, and it concerns the forethought of God. The Bible clearly teaches that believers are not merely "afterthoughts" of God, but forethoughts. This means that before God thought of or outlined any other part of His creation, He had us on His mind as being a part of the corporate Christ (the Church and Body of Jesus). The apostle Paul put it this way:

> *For whom He did foreknow, He also did predestinate to be conformed to the image of His Son, that He might be the firstborn among many brethren. Moreover whom He did predestinate, them He also called: and whom He called, them He also justified:*

> *and whom He justified, them He also glorified* (Romans 8:29-30).

> *Blessed be the God and Father of our Lord Jesus Christ, who hath blessed us with all spiritual blessings in heavenly places in Christ: According as he hath chosen us in him before the foundation of the world, that we should be holy and without blame before him in love: Having predestinated us unto the adoption of children by Jesus Christ to himself, according to the good pleasure of his will,* **(Ephesians 1:3-5).**

Both of these texts prove that you and I, as Christians, were predestinated in Christ before the foundation of the world. Some argue that the predestination refers only to the spiritual, and that it has little, if any, to do with the natural aspect of our lives. I have to respectfully disagree. I believe that the Scriptures teach that predestination and "Divine determination" each apply to both the spiritual and natural because we are spirit beings who have been eternally united with Jesus Christ as His Church.

According to Romans 8:29, the same God who foreknew our acceptance of the gospel from the beginning of time, also predestined us to be conformed to the image of His dear Son. That image is in spirit, mind, and character. Our spirits have already been regenerated, but our minds are being renewed and transformed daily as the very character and life of Christ is being cultivated in us.

What about the natural? Where does predestination or "Divine determination" fit in? I believe and will seek to prove by the Scriptures that God is the One who determines the sex, race, and other natural aspects of a person's life—

not mere chance.

Why is this so important? People practice bigotry and racism against other people who have no power or choice about their gender or race. If this was determined by God, who made everyone in accordance to His Divine will, then no finite being is qualified to judge or criticize God's creative genius concerning the natural makeup of individual human beings.

> *The Lord hath made all things for himself: yea, even the wicked for the day of evil* (Proverbs 16:4).

> *Nay but, O man, who art thou that repliest against God? Shall the thing formed say to him that formed it, Why hast thou made me thus?* (Romans 9:20)

I am learning to tell folks who have a problem with my race, color, or gender, "Take it up with my Creator, for I am His masterpiece! I am His one-of-a-kind Divine design." I have come to understand that I am not a Christian who just happens to be an African-American. I am a Christian who was predestined to be an African-American by Divine determination.

Therefore, I make no apology or excuse for my ethnicity. I believe that even though we are going to get new immortal and celestial bodies minus the defects and imperfections we have in these earthly tabernacles, our new bodies will be similar if not identical in appearance to the bodies we have now. Since Jesus is our example, these Scriptures confirm my belief:

> *Jesus saith unto her, Touch me not; for I am not yet ascended to my Father: but go to my brethren, and say unto them, I ascend unto my Father, and your Father; and to my God, and your God. Then the same day at evening, being the first day of the week, when the doors were shut where the disciples were assembled for fear of the Jews, came Jesus and stood in the midst, and saith unto them, Peace be unto you. And when he had so said, he shewed unto them his hands and his side. Then were the disciples glad, when they saw the Lord (John 20:17, 19-20).*
>
> *After these things Jesus shewed himself again to the disciples at the sea of Tiberias;... Now when Simon Peter heard that it was the Lord, he girt his fisher's coat unto him, (for he was naked,) and did cast himself into the sea (John 21:1,7).*

In each of these incidents, the disciples were able to recognize Jesus in His glorified state. Therefore, we have to believe that even though the Lord had already experienced a transformation from His mortal existence to immortality, He looked pretty much the same as He did before the change! Listen, I think that we might as well get used to the way we look now. Apart from scars caused by accidents, birth defects, obesity, or other alterations in your appearance (which came about by unnatural causes such as plastic surgery), you are going to look basically the same—if Jesus' experience is any indication of what is to come.

The bottom line is that God did not make a mistake when He made you to look like you do. He gave you the nose, eyes, height, and hair that He wanted you to have. To change or tamper with that is to insult and reject the creativity of God, who made you unique, a one-of-a-kind Divine design. When Jesus comes, He is not going to alter your appearance; only the substance and quality of your composition will be changed.

> *For our conversation is in heaven; from whence also we look for the Saviour, the Lord Jesus Christ: Who shall change our vile body, that it may be fashioned like unto his glorious body, according to the working whereby he is able even to subdue all things unto himself* **(Philippians 3:20-21).**

Who told you that you "did not look right" anyway? Who has the right and authority to classify your unique and distinguishing racial features as ugly and inferior? God surely did not! He doesn't fail, and He has declared that His creation is "very good"! (See Genesis 1:31) Any other opinion is the opinion of a liar!

Don't listen to the jealous and rebellious voice of bigotry, racism, and narrow mindedness uttering derogatory things about you! Learn to feel good about yourself. Appreciate the way God made you, and don't wait for others to accept or approve of you before you can begin to appreciate your own beauty and uniqueness.

Once you learn to love, appreciate, and recognize your own God-given beauty, worth, and uniqueness, others will have no other alternative but to do the same in time! I am humbled by the fact that God knew and ordained me to the ministry even as He did Jeremiah in days of old (Jeremiah 1:6-7). In fact, He not only predestined my calling, but He also divinely determined my race and sex as well! This is not just true for you and I, but for all who are called by His name.

The Christians who believe that the races should not mix in a congregational way here on earth will be in for a big shock in Heaven. The Book of Revelation makes it clear that there is no racism or segregation in Heaven. Ironically, although we all will belong to one race (the Christian race), there will still be ethnic and cultural diversity!

God's Kingdom is clearly based on "the salad bowl' concept, where all of its distinct elements bring in their unique qualities to comprise the whole. God isn't interested in dissolving everyone's uniqueness into nothingness—that is the nonsense of "nirvana" and the Eastern religions.

And they sung a new song, saying, Thou art worthy to take the book, and to open the seals thereof: for thou wast slain, and hast redeemed us to God by thy blood out of every kindred, and tongue, and people, and nation; And hast made us unto our God kings and priests: and we shall reign on the earth (Revelation 5:9-10).

After this I beheld, and, lo, a great multitude, which no man could number, of all nations, and kindreds, and people, and tongues, stood before the throne, and beforethe Lamb, clothed with white robes, and palms in their hands; And cried with a loud voice, saying, Salvation to our God which sitteth upon the throne, and unto the Lamb (Revelation 7:9-10).

It should be clear that your ethnicity and gender was a definite act of God, and not blind chance or a mistake. God chose to make you the color that you are, and He gave you the features that you have and placed you in the race that you belong to. He stands by His decision and will not flinch an inch simply because you are dissatisfied or want to be like someone else. He will not budge just because you have allowed someone's irrational racist remarks to make you feel inferior, insulted, or ugly.

You are beautiful and accepted in His sight, so the opinions and words of others should not matter! His righteousness has exalted you from the ugly slums of degeneracy and removed all fear, guilt, intimidation, and inferiority. The Father declares and sees you as being equal with Christ! I emphasize this because all of us—Caucasian or African-American —need to alter the way we see and deal with one another. White believers who may still be afflicted by a superiority complex toward African-Americans need to be more sober in their estimates of their own worth. The opposite is true for most African Americans that suffer from the inferiority mind-sets created by generations of slavery and systematic racism, segregation, and discrimination. This type of low self-esteem is extremely difficult to dismantle. The main thing to remember about our race, color, or sex is that God predestined us to be the way we are!

When every believer comes to openly accept the ethnicity or personal characteristics of other believers without partiality or bias, then the wall of racism will collapse because its very foundation will dissolve!

My brethren, have not the faith of our Lord Jesus Christ, the Lord of glory, with respect of persons. If ye fulfil the royal law according to the scripture, Thou shalt love thy neighbour as thyself, ye do well: But if e have respect to persons, ye commit sin, and are convinced of the law as transgressors (James 2:1, 8-9).

For ye are all the children of God by faith in Christ Jesus. For as many of you as have been baptized into Christ have put on Christ. There is neither Jew nor Greek, there is neither bond nor free, there is neither male nor female: for ye are all one in Christ Jesus (Galatians 3:26-28).

CHAPTER EIGHT
Interracial Marriages in the Church: Are They Scripturally Consistent?

And Adam said, This is now bone of my bones, and flesh of my flesh: she shall be called Woman, because she was taken out of Man (Genesis 2:23).

Whoso findeth a wife findeth a good thing, and obtaineth favour of the Lord (Proverbs 18:22).

Marriage is honourable in all, and the bed undefiled: but whoremongers and adulterers God will judge (Hebrews 13:4).

One of the greatest fears in the Church by professing Christians is that of, "racial mixing" (miscegenation), or interracial marriages. I use the term professing Christians because these individuals have a form of godliness and do not allow the scripture to be the final authority in the matter of race relations. The overwhelming majority of Christians who have these fears about interracial marriages are Caucasian. They fear the union of Caucasians with African-Americans, Asians, Latinos, and any people group that don't match their complexion or culture. Concerning

African-Americans, much of this fear stems from a lie devised by Caucasian bigots prior to the Civil War! Claiming that males of African descent were "bucks" with animal-like sexual tendencies and abilities, these racists justified these lies under the supposed necessity to protect and preserve the sanctity of Caucasian females from the exaggerated sexual prowess of African-American men.

The Bible says something entirely different about this issue of interracial marriage. Our goal is to rightly divide the Word, bypassing our personal fears, traditions, biases, and opinions (see 2nd Corinthians 4:2; 2nd Timothy 2:15; Revelation 22:19).

One of the greatest scholars and theologians to emerge from the Pentecostal/Charismatic circle was Finis Jennings Dake. He compiled *Dake's Annotated Reference Bible*, which, in my estimation, is the greatest reference Bible ever put together. It is the first of its kind to be compiled by a scholar and theologian of the Pentecostal circle. It deals with important issues and doctrines from more of a Full Gospel, Charismatic, and Pentecostal perspective. I have benefited tremendously from the historical facts, references, and comments in its pages.

The book's one glaring weakness appears in a special section entitled, "Notes on the Books of Acts"[6], which includes a list that is titled, "Thirty Reasons for Segregation of Races". Although I believe that Mr. Dakes' overall work is commendable and even excellent, in the area of race relations, his findings were tainted by a strong racial bias.

Time and space limitations make it impossible for me to refute each of the 30 reasons Dake provides for the segregation of races, but I will seek to disprove the most important claims by presenting a clear witness from God's Word. You must be the judge.

1. God wills all races to be as He made them. Any violation of God's original purpose manifests insubordination to Him.

God does will all races to be as He made them and not to feel inadequate or inferior to others of diverse ethnicity.

However, to say or suggest that interracial marriages are acts of defiance and insubordination to God's purpose is racially motivated. (*Satan uses this to keep God's people divided*). This statement reflects a blatant disregard of the biblical and historical record! Many important interracial marriages took place by God's direct plan and other, and most of these unions involved the Messiah!

2. God made everything to reproduce after his own kind.

Mr. Dake again missed the mark of "rightly dividing" the Word, which is uncharacteristic of him. The word kind appears repeatedly in the Book of Genesis. The word means "species" in every case, but Mr. Dake said, "kind means type and color." In all due respect, that is not exactly an accurate definition of that word. *Young's Analytical Concordance to the Bible, Wilson's Old Testament Word Studies, James Strong's The Exhaustive Concordance of the Bible,* and many other very reliable and authoritative sources define this Hebrew word, min, to mean "species." Negroes, Mongolians, Caucasians, and other ethnic groups are not distinct species, but ethnic divisions of the human species. The apostle Paul seal the issue with divine authority: "All flesh is not the same flesh: *but there is one kind of flesh of men,* another flesh of beasts, another of fishes, and another of "birds" (1st Corinthians 15:39).

3. God cursed angels for leaving their own first estate and their own habitation to marry the daughters of men.

Racial segregation to avoid miscegenation has nothing to do with the fact that God cursed the angels who left their first estate and habitation to marry the daughters of men, as Mr. Dake proposed.

If the scriptural account of the "sons of God" in Genesis 6:1-4 describes the union of women with angels, then it reveals a clear violation of the law of separation of species. If the "sons of God" are actually men, then no violation occurred. In any case, the Bible doesn't show disapproval since punishments was not prescribed in that passage. It is simply noted that the offspring of the unions were called "mighty men" on the earth. The sin that brought the destruction of the flood came later.

The phrase, "angels who left their first estate and habitation," comes from Bible references in the Old and New Testaments, and it refers to the one-third of the angels of Heaven who joined satan's revolt against the Almighty. They instantly lost the privileges of their "first estate" and were cast out of their heavenly "habitation." Nowhere is it tied to the "sons of God" mentioned in Genesis 6. One of my spiritual mentors taught me, "When the plain sense of Scripture makes common sense, then seek no other sense. The Word makes sense.

4. Even in heaven certain groups will not be allowed to worship together

Mr. Dake cited Revelation 7:7-17, 14:1-5, and 15:2-5 as the scriptural basis for his assertion, but these make it clear that there was no attempt made to keep ethnic groups from worshiping together. The first passage cited by Mr. Dakes declares, "After this I beheld, and lo, a great multitude, which no man could number, *of all nations, and kindreds, and people, and tongues,* stood before the throne, and before the Lamb, clothed with white robes, and palms in their hands" (Revelations 7:9).

It is absurd, misleading, and downright deceptive to think or teach that segregation is condoned or practiced in any shape, form, or fashion in Heaven! Some Bible passages depict various groups of believers worshiping God separately during the time of Jacob's trouble (see Jeremiah 30:7; Daniel 12:1), but this certainly does not prove that segregation will be practiced in Heaven in regard to worship. Heaven is a place of unity and harmony:

> *For this cause I bow my knees unto the Father of our Lord Jesus Christ, of whom the whole family in heaven and earth is named,* (Ephesians 3:14-15).

5. Segregation was so strong in the Old Testament that an ox and an ass could not be worked together (see Deuteronomy 22:10).

If your culture still uses donkeys and oxen to plow or pull freight, then don't yoke the two species together, but don't be fooled into believing that this verse applies to interracial marriages. Just as this verse has nothing to do with males and females working together (they are the same species, but they have different temperaments and natures), neither does it have to do with different races of human beings coming together! This Scripture was not an "allegory" to substantiate segregating the races, it was simply good, "common sense" advice on how to work animals effectively.

6. *When two people of diverse races marry, they are unequally yoked.*

This final claim is raised by many Christians who oppose mixed marriages, especially those between African-American and Caucasians. They often quote the apostle Paul to support their position:

Be ye not unequally yoked together with unbelievers: for what fellowship hath righteousness with unrighteousness? and what communion hath light with darkness? (2nd **Corinthians 6:14**)

How can this passage be used to ban marriages between Christians who have different skin tones? The apostle Paul was warning Christian believers against the dangers of having fellowship with unbelievers and infidels—not other blood-washed believers! (See First Corinthians 15:33.) His warning had nothing to do with skin color or ethnicity; he was concerned about spiritual citizenship.

Most people who oppose interracial marriage oppose Caucasians marrying African-Americans more than anything else. Mr. Dake confirmed his own concern in "The Acts of the Apostles," Column 1, Reason 4 (page 159): *"Miscegenation means the mixtures of races, especially the black and white races, or those of outstanding type of color."* The real root of opposition to interracial marriages in the Church is not scriptural; it is purely racist. It stems from ignorance, fear, ethnic pride, and a racial superiority complex. Sadly, it is deeply rooted in the history of this nation, going all the way back to when the first Africans were brought to this land as slaves.

As an African-American, I am proud of my heritage. Through God's Word, I have learned that I was fearfully and wonderfully created to be equal with all men. I am not ashamed of my dark complexion, my kinky hair, or any of my other distinguishing Negroid features. When my daughter and my son marry, I naturally want their children to resemble me in some way. It is natural that I hope they marry someone who will be able to help produce that desire.

However, as a Christian, I refuse to allow my preference to make me racist or biased if they choose spouses from races or ethnic groups other than African-Americans. My greatest desire, requirement, and prayer is:

a. regardless of their skin or color, let their nature be divine (see 2nd Peter 1:4)

b. let their character be Christ-like,

c. and let their attitude be one of humility and gratitude.

Interracial Marriages in Scripture

Therefore I esteem all thy precepts concerning all things to be right; and I hate every false way (Psalm 119:128).

To the law and to the testimony: if they speak not according to this word, it is because there is no light in them (Isaiah 8:20).

> *For whatsoever things were written aforetime were written for our learning, that we through patience and comfort of the scriptures might have hope* (Romans 15:4).

> *All scripture is given by inspiration of God, and is profitable for doctrine, for reproof, for correction, for instruction in righteousness:* (2nd Timothy 3:16).

You may wonder why I use so many Scriptures in my teachings and writings. The answer is that I have always been a stickler for the Word of God because I firmly believe that the most effective way to explain things, especially topics of a biblical nature, is with the Word itself. Every issue must be measured and framed by the Word of God. In my discussion on racism, *if I fail to produce precedent and proof from the Scriptures,* then my argument is merely opinionated and theoretical rhetoric. However, I do have some scriptural precedents and proof that interracial marriages are permissible. In fact, God himself orchestrated a few!

Abraham and Hagar

> *And Sarai Abram's wife took Hagar her maid the Egyptian, after Abram had dwelt ten years in the land of Canaan, and gave her to her husband Abram to be his wife* (Genesis 16:3).

The union between Abraham and Hagar was not necessarily the perfect plan of God. However, even though Abraham blundered by following the advice of his wife,

Sarah, God meant it for good. The child Hagar bore Abram fulfilled God's promise that *nations* would come from Abraham's loins (see Genesis 17:6, 20). Abram's union with Hagar is one of the first interracial marriages recorded in the Bible. Hagar was an Egyptian, descended from Ham. She became the mother of Ishmael, from which the Arab nations are descended.

Moses and Zipporah

And Moses was content to dwell with the man: and he gave Moses Zipporah his daughter (Exodus 2:21).

And Miriam and Aaron spake against Moses because of the Ethiopian woman whom he had married: for he had married an Ethiopian woman (Numbers 12:1).

Some opponents of interracial marriages are forced to argue that Zipporah was not a woman of African descent, because if they accept the fact that Moses was married to an African woman—as I believe the Scriptures pointedly portray her—then their racist arguments completely collapse for lack of scriptural support! Their "theological racism" disregards, denies, and distorts the prominent role that people of African descent have played in biblical history.

Most respected Hebrews scholars agree that Zipporah was of African descent. The term *Ethiopian* is generally ascribed to the descendants of Cush and Ham. It is clear that the marriage of Moses and Zipporah was an interracial marriage, and it was clearly *orchestrated by God* that His purpose might be fulfilled! It was God who led Moses to the camp of Jethro (also called Jether and Reuel, the "friend of

God") so he could learn how to be a shepherd, and so he could meet God face to face on the mountain of Horeb.

Salmon and Rahab

And Joshua the son of Nun sent out of Shittim two men to spy secrectly, saying, Go view the land, even Jericho And they went, and came into an harlot's house, named Rahab, and lodged there (Joshua 2:1).

And Joshua saved Rahab the harlot alive, and her father's household, and all that she had; and she dwelleth in Israel even unto this day; because she hid the messengers, which Joshua sent to spy out Jericho (Joshua 6:25).

The book of the generation of Jesus Christ, the son of David, the son of Abraham. Abraham begat Issac... And Salmon begat Booz of Rachab; and Booz begat Obed of Ruth; and Obed begat Jesse; (Matthew 1:1-2,5).

The union of Salmon and Rahab was another interracial marriage that was orchestrated by God. Salmon, a Shemitic man, and Rahab, a Hamatic woman, produced Boaz, an ancestor of David and Jesus Christ! If God is opposed to interracial marriages, as Mr. Dake and others claim, then why did He select a woman of another race to be the progenitor and direct ancestor of His Son, the Messiah?

Boaz and Ruth

And Elimelech Naomi's husband died; and she was left, and her two sons. And they took them wives of the women of Moab; the name of the one was Orpah, and the name of the other Ruth: and they dwelled there about ten years.

And Mahlon and Chilion died also both of them; and the woman was left of her two sons and her husband. Then she arose with her daughters in law, that she might return from the country of Moab: for she had heard in the country of Moab how that the Lord had visited his people in giving them bread (Ruth 1:3-6).

And Boaz said unto the elders, and unto all the people, Ye are witnesses this day, that I have bought all that was Elimelech's, and all that was Chilion's and Mahlon's, of the hand of Naomi. Moreover Ruth the Moabitess, the wife of Mahlon, have I purchased to be my wife, to raise up the name of the dead upon his inheritance, that the name of the dead be not cut off from among his brethren, and from the gate of his place: ye are witnesses this day. So Boaz took Ruth, and she was his wife: and when he went in unto her, the Lord gave her conception, and she bare a son. And the women her neighbours gave it a name, saying, There is a son born to Naomi; and they called his name Obed: he is the father of Jesse, the father of David (Ruth 4:9-10, 13, 17).

Both Mahlon and Boaz were from a different ethnic background than Ruth, which disapproves the teaching that interracial marriages are scripturally wrong. God orchestrated this interracial marriage between an Israelite and a Moabitess, and He gave them a son named Obed, the father of Jesse and the grandfather of David.

David and Bathsheba

And when the wife of Uriah heard that Uriah her husband was dead, she mourned for her husband. And when the mourning was past, David sent and fetched her to his house, and she became his wife and bare him a son. But the thing that David had done displeased the Lord (2nd Samuel 11:26-27).

And David comforted Bathsheba his wife, and went in unto her, and lay with her: and she bare a son, and he called his name Solomon: and the Lord loved him (2nd Samuel 12:24).

Despite the negative aspects surrounding the initial relationship of David and Bathsheba, we have to conclude that God had predestined this union from the foundation of the world because of the offspring it produced. Solomon was a direct ancestor of Jesus Christ. The union of David and Bathsheba was an interracial marriage that was orchestrated, or at the very least, blessed by God. Bathsheba was not an Israelite, because her first husband, Uriah, was a Hittite of the Hamitic (black) ancestry. The Hittites were descendants of Ham's grandson Heth, who was the son of Canaaan (see Genesis 10:15).

Eunice and Timothy's Greek Father

Then came he (Paul) to Derbe and Lystra: and,

> *behold, a certain disciple was there, named Timotheus (Timothy), the son of a certain woman, which was a Jewess, and believed; but his father was a Greek:* (Acts 16:1).

Timothy was the offspring of an interracial marriage. Although the name of Timothy's father has been omitted from Scripture, I am fully convinced that the union of Timothy's Jewish mother to his Gentile father was not a mere coincidence, but an orchestration of divine purpose to produce Timothy, who played such a key role in the development of the early Church!

The Sword of the Spirit has sliced away the distortions, deceptions, and unscriptural biases that have been mustered by men who oppose interracial marriages. The bottom line to this whole matter is that God gives every man and woman the right to choose a suitable and complementary companion. Your choice doesn't have to meet my expectations, nor does my choice have to meet your requirements. The only valid question is: *Does the prospective companion meet God's expectations and requirements?* Race is not a factor with God, for He looks at the heart.

CHAPTER NINE
True Confession of a Once Racist Black Man

Now I want to consider someone whom I know better than anyone else in the world as we retrace the steps I had to take to overcome a racist attitude.

The racism and bigotry that was bottled up in me was ignited by the discrimination I experienced and the offenses I endured as a victim of a racist system. My racism was reactionary or reverse in nature. From my beginning days as an infant to the day of my spiritual emancipation (which occurred somewhere in my early twenties), *I was brainwashed.*

How was I brainwashed? I was brainwashed by the words, actions, policies, personal and institutional rejections, official decisions, and the cultural environment of a discriminatory and racially biased educational system. My sense of value was unceasingly assaulted by the media, by the judicial system, by the political system, and even by the Church! I was continually taught and reminded in every area of my childhood and adolescence that because I was an African-American, I was inferior and not equal to Caucasians.

I accepted this concept with little resistance. The only exceptions were those times my mother encouraged me by telling me that I was just as important as anybody else. *Thank God for Mama!* I have to credit my father for a lot of the anger and defiance that began to boil in me regarding our racist community during my adolescent years.

It seems like I reached puberty in more ways than one as I watched my father repeatedly take a stand against certain Caucasian men who tried to use their color to intimidate and take advantage of him. Back then; he was perhaps one of the first African-American men in our town to break away from Caucasian employers to form his own crew of workers. Looking back, I think I took his accomplishments for granted. I really didn't recognize or appreciate his role in helping to shape my life and character.

I will never forget one particular incident that made a lasting impact on my life. One of the leading Caucasian general contractors in our area had a record for harassing, intimidating, and swindling African-American people who worked for him, and even those he did work for. The day came when this man brushed my father the wrong way.

We were laying bricks for this man, who was also under contract to build us a house. For some reason, the man had stalled and stopped construction altogether on our house, and for no legitimate reason. We were busy laying bricks (for a whole lot less than what our Caucasian counterparts were getting back then), when "Mr. M" drove up. I had witnessed manifestations of my father's anger against other African-American men when they had pushed too hard, but I had never actually seen him face down a Caucasian man (especially one of this caliber).

The two men began to talk, and when Mr. M said something that upset my father, one thing led to another.

Finally I heard Dad shout, "I am a man too, and you know you can't beat me!" At this point, Mr. M knew he had to either "put up or shut up!" There was just no way that this out-of-shape man, who was accustomed to others (African-American in particular) doing his work for him, could match the physical prowess of this 210-pound muscular African-American man who knew how to rumble!

Mr. M's bluff had been called, so he did the rational thing. He quickly backed down, got in his car, and left. Things would never be the same from that day forward—especially for me. I had seen my father, a African-American man, overcome the intimidating racist tactics of a Caucasian bigot. The impossible had become possible.

That incident took place in the turbulence of the mid-1960, and the tide of "black awareness" and defiance was rising. The winds of change and protest were sweeping America and highlighting the plight of the African-American community. Even remote and isolated places like my hometown of Dillon, South Carolina, were beginning to feel a breeze from the storm that was raging in other areas.

During this eight-year season of change, I was emancipated from the inferiority complex that years of racism had developed in me. In fact, I went from one extreme to another, and I literally began to despise all Caucasian people. In 1971, I attended college in Springfield, Massachusetts, and for the first time spent lengthy periods away from home.

I had a baptism of fire into a world that I had only imagined or dreamed of. I met many other young African-Americans who thought, talked, and felt like me about their "blackness." They were audacious, articulate, and angry. I thought this type of atmosphere suited me well. The anger and resentment toward Caucasian people that had been bottled up in me reached its boiling point on this campus filled with racial tension and confrontation.

I learned the hard way that certain parts of the North were just as racist as the South. Springfield was one of those places in those days. However, what made the difference was that African-Americans up there were not as complacent, ill informed, or intimidated by Caucasians. They were not afraid to speak out or protest injustices. This was especially true on college campuses. That year was a time of learning, and my convictions were confirmed about my heritage and the plight of Americans.

After summer break, I did not return to school. I made plans to transfer to a college closer to home, but unknown to me; my plans were about to be overturned by Divine determination. For some reason that I did not understanding then, my desire to return to school and finish my education left me. I convinced myself that I would eventually go back, but never did. I married the young lady who now shares the ministry with me instead.

We had it rough because I had convinced myself that I was too smart to work for any Caucasian man. I worked with my father and brothers as a bricklayer for a while, but I couldn't commit myself to it because my mind was always somewhere else. My negligence as a husband and provider put a strain on our marriage, and ironically, that made me even angrier about the racist system I felt had trapped me.

I tried to justify my failures by shifting the blame onto the Caucasian man. I became so distraught with the system and embittered with my own reactionary racism and hatred that I seriously thought about bombing a prestigious Caucasian church! While I was in this confused and embittered state, I was almost ensnared by the tentacles of Islam because I had seen hypocrisy and racial discrimination in many Caucasians that confessed to be Christians.

All this may sound foolish and fictitious now, but I am telling the truth. I was so angry with Caucasian people that my whole character and creative expression, as seen through the poems, novels, and other materials I wrote then, reflected the gall of bitterness and racism that I had allowed to infest my total being.

From Confrontation to Emancipation

Things seemed to get worse for me in nearly every area of life as my anger continued to grow. I didn't realize it at the time, but I was about to have a confrontation with God that would completely alter the course of my life. My first pastor had spoken anointed words of prophecy over me when I was very young, and my mother and others maintained a constant prayer vigil over me because of my defiant attitude toward authority and my crumbling marriage.

I was way out on a limb, using drugs and meddling in the occult and sexual promiscuity. I even perpetrated theft and armed robbery. I had reached the bottom of the barrel, sinking to the very level of lewdness that I had despised in others. Nevertheless, it was in the belly of the whale of racism that I truly met God for the first time.

After a failed attempt to hold up a salesman at gunpoint in my own yard, I could not take it any more. I remember falling on my knees in my little mobile home while I was alone. When I tearfully asked God to forgive me and take control of my life, it seemed like nothing happened. My emotions didn't seem to conform to the erroneous things I'd been taught about "being saved" in my legalistic and religious upbringing. Praise God, the seed of my redemption had been planted and nothing that the devil, the flesh, or the world could do would keep it from germinating.

My deliverance from sin and racism came a few weeks later in an old-fashioned revival held at my home church. The Word of God and the Holy Spirit completely devastated me that night. I was broken and put back together again. I was emptied and refilled. My heart of stone, which had been filled with bitterness, hatred, and racism, was melted by His presence, and then God replaced it with a heart of flesh, love, and compassion. I remember going to a certain woman who was present whom I thought was Caucasian (she was actually half-Indian and Caucasian) and saying to her in tears of joy, "I love everybody! I love you and I don't hate Caucasian people any more!" She looked at me in amazement, no doubt wondering what my motive was and what that statement meant.

If she had only known the depth of my bitterness and resentment toward light-skinned people like herself, she would have understood my tears, my words, and my victory celebration. I can truly say that I have remained free from the power of racism ever since that night.

"*If the Son therefore shall make you free, ye shall be free indeed*" *(John 8:36).*

Although I was now free of my hatred toward other races, I quickly learned that all the people who professed to be born-again Christians had not necessarily been delivered from their racial attitudes as I had. This fact bothered me for years after my conversion and consequent deliverance from racism. I was shocked to see so much racism in the Church.

At one point, I tried to evade the issue and lived in a state of pretense and denial. "After all", I thought, "I am saved now, and racism is a natural matter for natural people to contend with." I quickly learned that racism is a sin that not only divides this nation, but the Church as well.

Racism is a disgraceful and detestable evil that prevents the Body of Christ from coming into the unity of the faith. It pits spiritual brothers against spiritual brothers. I am convinced that God is so grieved and angered over racism that He is at the point of pronouncing judgment upon those who will not judge themselves and repent of this sin.

Far too much is a stake. He will not allow us to remain in our little segregated corners or cling to our fleshly traditions and concepts that exalt themselves against the Word of God. Something is coming down, and I assure you that it will not be the counsel of God!

The Lord bringeth the counsel of the heathen to nought: he maketh the devices of the people of none effect. The counsel of the Lord standeth for ever, the thoughts of his heart to all generations (Psalm 33:10-11).

Chapter Ten
Prophecy Demands the Defeat of Racism in the Church Before the Return of Jesus

Many Christians believe that The Rapture and Second Coming of Christ are imminent and could occur at any time. They also believe that there is absolutely no unfulfilled prophecy in Scripture that would prevent this literal and inevitable event (The Rapture) from happening at any time.

I once held that opinion, and I developed an escapist mentality concerning "the end times." However, as I studied the Word in more depth and detail, I became convinced that prophecy requires that certain things must happen in the world and Church before The Rapture and Second Coming transpire.

The Word of God is being fulfilled all around us in regard to the gross darkness and degeneracy that has engulfed the world. Bible prophecy is also being fulfilled in the Church, in both negative and positive ways. Some are departing from the faith while others are drawing close to God. Some are selling out to selfish motivations and ambitions while others are selling out to God, thus bringing the Kingdom in its fullness.

The Bible declares that two things must happen before the rapture or second coming can take place. Both of these things are directly related to the problem of racism. I call these prophetic events "The Two Untils." The word *until* is important because it "connects, yet separates" the events that precede and precipitate the main event of our Lord's return.

Until We All Come Into Unity

It is unscriptural to think that the rapture will take place before a "necessary number" of Christians of diverse denominational and racial backgrounds come into unity and fellowship. Jesus personally substantiated this fact of prophecy:

> *I am the good shepherd, and know My sheep, and am known of Mine. As the Father knoweth Me, even so know I the Father: and I lay down My life for the sheep. And other sheep I have, which are not of this fold: them also I must bring, and they shall hear My voice; and there shall be one fold, and one shepherd* (John 10:14-16).

> *Neither pray I for these alone, but for them also which shall believe on Me through their word; that they all may be one; as Thou, Father, art in Me, and I in Thee that they also may be one in Us: that the world may believe that Thou hast sent Me. And the glory which Thou gavest Me I have given them; that they may be one, even as We are one: I in them, and Thou in Me, that they may be made perfect in one; and that the world may know that Thou hast sent Me, and hast loved them, as Thou hast loved Me* (John 17:20-23).

Anyone who disputes or denies that unity is not only a *desire* but also a *demand* of our Lord for His Church may be contributing to the problem of disunity by inadvertently causing dissension and division. How is this desire and prayer of Jesus Christ for unity in His Church being fulfilled? The apostle Paul penned the answer in his letter to the church at Ephesus:

> *And He gave some, apostles; and some, prophets; and some, evangelists; and some, pastors and teachers; for the perfecting of the saints, for the work of the ministry, for the edifying of the body of Christ: Till we all come in the unity of the faith, and of the knowledge of the Son of God, unto a perfect man, unto the measure of the stature of the fullness of Christ: that we henceforth be no more children, tossed to and fro, and carried about with every wind of doctrine, by the sleight of men, and cunning craftiness, whereby they lie in wait to deceive; but speaking the truth in love, may grow up into Him in all things, which is the head, even Christ: from whom the whole body fitly joined together and compacted by that which every joint supplieth, according to the effectual working in the measure of every part, maketh increase of the body unto the edifying of itself in love (Ephesians 4:11-16).*

Did you see Paul's inspired statement about the "unity of the faith" in the thirteenth verse? This statement and many others make it clear that The Rapture of the Church is contingent on it coming into the unity of the faith! The Lord is coming back for a glorious and unified Church. Principle or theory just will not do; we must have unity in practice. Many things must happen to achieve this state of unity in the universal Church.

It is vitally important that we abolish racist attitudes, concepts, policies and practices among the remnant of true Christians and local churches to achieve unity in the eyes of God. Until we accomplish this in accordance with our Father's Word, we are like birds without wings that long to fly up and away, but are doomed to stay earthbound.

Until His Enemies Be Made His Footstool

Why did the Father declare He would subdue the enemies of Jesus and put them under His feet before The Rapture takes place? Who are His enemies and what constitutes His feet in the earth? The second "until" is predicated upon the following Scripture passage:

> *This Jesus hath God raised up, whereof we all are witnesses. Therefore being by the right hand of God exalted, and having received of the Father the promise of the Holy Ghost, he hath shed forth this, which ye now see and hear. For David is not ascended into the heavens: but he saith himself, The Lord said unto my Lord, Sit Thou on My right hand, until I make Thy foes Thy footstool. Therefore let all the house of Israel know assuredly, that God hath made the same Jesus, Whom ye have crucified, both Lord and Christ (Acts 2:32-36).*

It is clear that Jesus is going to remain where He is—at the right hand of the Father—until the Father makes His enemies His footstool. I believe we are seeing a gradual and two-fold fulfillment of this prophecy. First, God will deal with the enemies of Jesus within the Church, for judgment must begin at the house of God! (See 1st Peter 4:17.) This has begun, and it will only accelerate and intensify in the coming days! The enemies among us and in us must be subdued and they are not always evil spirits as most suppose. We have given the devil far too much credit for the degeneracy and rebellion that we ourselves contain and nurture in our flesh.

Though the Bible clearly calls the devil our enemy (see 1st Peter 5:8), he cannot be blamed or credited for every adversity or affliction in our lives. God permits these things at times to perfect us, to try our faith, and to work out His purposes in our lives (see Psalm 66:10-12; 119:70, 75). Adversity and affliction is often caused by our own sin and rebellion (see 1st Peter 2.20; 4:15).

Racism is one enemy and affliction that was birthed and reared to maturity in the Church through the evil that lurks among us and in us. We must subdue racism and place it under the feet and authority of Jesus, our Lord and King. The Apostle Paul wrote about a second phase in this process and subduing our Lord's enemies and placing them under His feet. It specifically concerns the nations and the world system:

> *Then cometh the end, when He shall have delivered up the kingdom to God, even the Father; when He shall have put down all rule and all authority and power. For He must reign, till He hath put all enemies under his feet. The last enemy that shall be destroyed is death.*

For He hath put all things under His feet. But when He saith all things are put under Him, it is manifest that He is excepted which did put all things under Him. And when all things shall be subdued unto Him, then shall the Son also Himself be subject unto Him that put all things under Him, that God may be all in all (1st Corinthians 15:24-28).

Do not forget that the enemies of the cross have won themselves a foothold in the internal structure of the Church. They must be exposed, subdued, and brought under His feet before The Rapture can take place. I believe the Scriptures confirm that the Church is the Body of Christ, and our feet will tread down every enemy.

Then David the king stood up upon his feet, and said, Hear me, my brethren, and my people: As for me, I had in mine heart to build an house of rest for the ark of the covenant of the Lord, and for the footstool of our God, and had made ready for the building (1st Chronicles 28:2).

We will go into His tabernacles: we will worship at His footstool (Psalm 132:7).

The glory of Lebanon shall come unto thee, the fir tree, the pine tree, and the box together, to beautify the place of My sanctuary; and I will make the place of My feet glorious (Isaiah 60:13).

And hath put all things under His feet, and gave Him to be the head over all things to the church, which is His body, the fulness of him that filleth all in all (Ephesians 1:22-23).

These passages confirm that we, in the Church, are the "feet" of Jesus, and that the Father is using us to put all of His enemies under His rule. I am excited because I am convinced that the army that God is raising up in this final hour will subdue every enemy of the cross, regardless of its nature or name! When the battle is over and the victory has been won, the Commander-in-Chief shall summon us home to Glory.

CHAPTER ELEVEN
The Balm of Gilead: The Only Cure for Racism in the Church

Is there no balm in Gilead; is there no physician there? why then is not the health of the daughter of my people recovered? (Jeremiah 8:22)

We have considered the factors that infected the Church with racism, and the consequences of the disease for the Church and the world. Now we have to ask, "How can we be healed?"

There is a physician named Jesus who initiated the healing process at Calvary, and He has successfully "cured" many sick and wounded members of the Body like myself. Each of His patients from various racial and denominational backgrounds become a "human syringe" whom the Holy Spirit uses to "inoculate" the Body of Christ against the deadly virus of racism.

I believe that just as our Creator gave us natural antibodies to ward off disease and help our bodies heal themselves, so has He equipped the Body of Christ to heal itself of malignant diseases like racism. "Dear Lord, let the healing begin."

Twelve Practical Ways for Christians and Churches to Expose and Eliminate Racism.

1. See and Treat Racism as the Sin That It Is.

Then Peter opened his mouth, and said, Of a truth I perceive that God is no respecter of persons: (Acts 10:34).

My brethren, have not the faith of our Lord Jesus Christ, the Lord of glory, with respect of persons (James 2:1).

Many Christians are guilty of the sin of racism because they don't realize that bigotry is a sin. Their minds have been blurred by cultural traditions passed down from generation to generation. This is especially true for many Caucasian Southerners who were taught from infancy that they were superior to African-Americans.

Luke and James used Greek words with identical definitions that will help expose racism as the sin it is. In Acts 10:34, when Luke wrote, *"God is no respect of persons,"* he used the Greek word *prosopoleptes*. The translators of the Authorized Version translated it as respecter, but the Greek word literally means *"accepter of faces."* James used a similar word in James 2:9, and it means the same exact thing!

The term, *accepter of faces*, means to give preferential treatment to someone because of their race, sex, appearance, or socioeconomic status. Racism is any guise is ungodly unholy, and unrighteous. "All unrighteousness is sin" (1 John 5:17a).

2. Renounce and Repent of Prejudice and Racist Attitudes So You Can Help Free Others.

For with what judgment ye judge, ye shall be judged: and with what measure ye mete, it shall be measured to you again. Thou hypocrite, first cast out the beam out of thine own eye; and then shalt thou see clearly to cast out the mote out of thy brother's eye (Matthew 7:2,5).

For though we walk in the flesh, we do not war after the flesh: (For the weapons of our warfare are not carnal, but mighty through God to the pulling down of strong holds;) Casting down imaginations, and every high thing that exalteth itself against the knowledge of God, and bringing into captivity every thought to the obedience of Christ; (2nd Corinthians 10:3-5).

The Holy Spirit will never enlist someone who is still prejudiced and racist to address and attack the sin of racism. Yet there are strongholds of racism (fortresses made of thoughts) and imaginations (images) that have been planted in the minds of many believers as a result of generations of misconception, fear, and ignorance. They are not easily destroyed, but I thank God He has given us the inner fortitude to tear down these racist attitudes through Jesus Christ. If you want to please God more than man, then you can be released from the bondage of bigotry and begin to help free others by the Spirit.

3. Confront Every Form of Racism in Your Relationships.

> *But when Peter was come to Antioch, I withstood him to the face, because he was to be blamed. For before that certain came from James, he did eat with the Gentiles: but when they were come, he withdrew and separated himself, fearing them which were of the circumcision* (Galatians 2:11-12).

Paul's confrontation of Peter graphically illustrates the need to boldly "speak the truth in love" when brothers or sisters fail to follow God's Word (see Ephesians 4:15). Peter had overcome the prejudice and bigotry of his Judaic heritage, but he yielded to peer pressure. Paul obediently confronted Peter, and he restored truth to the Church. Would racism have flourished in the Church if some renowned or prominent leader had confronted others of equal credentials openly and publicly as Paul confronted Peter? I don't think so.

We need a courageous commitment to effectively resist racism in the Church today. Believers at every level of Church leadership must become bold enough to speak out in love against this evil sin. The Holy Spirit is dealing with Christian leaders in strategic places to boldly sound the trumpet against the sin of racism. This is not a day of compromise and cowardice, but of commitment and courage.

> *And thou, son of man, be not afraid of them, neither be afraid of their words, though briers and thorns be with thee, and thou dost dwell among scorpions: be not afraid of their words, nor be dismayed at their looks, though they be a rebellious house. And thou shalt speak my words unto them, whether they will hear, or whether they will forbear: for they are most rebellious* (Ezekiel 2:6-7).

4. See People as God Does and Refuse to Know Anyone After the Flesh.

But the Lord said unto Samuel, Look not on his countenance, or on the height of his stature; because I have refused him: for the Lord seeth not as man seeth; for man looketh on the outward appearance, but the Lord looketh on the heart (1st Samuel 16:7).

Wherefore henceforth know we no man after the flesh: yea, though we have known Christ after the flesh, yet now henceforth know we him no more. Therefore if any man be in Christ, he is a new creature: old things are passed away; behold, all things are become new (2nd Corinthians 5:16-17).

Paul told the saints in Corinth, "Henceforth know we no man after the flesh," only after the Spirit had purged away his personal prejudices and bigotry. He saw people as God does, and it demolished every trace of racism in his once partial mind. He also said:

There is neither Jew nor Greek, there is neither bond nor free, there is neither male nor female: for ye are all one in Christ Jesus (Galatians 3:28).

I used to hate Caucasian people with a passion, but I thank God that He supernaturally delivered me from the bitterness and unforgiveness of *reverse racism*. Like Paul, we need to see people as God does and seek to know no one after the flesh.

5. Accept Divinely Predetermined Individual Ethnic Uniqueness.

I will praise thee; for I am fearfully and wonderfully made: marvellous are thy works; and that my soul knoweth right well (Psalm 139:14).

Before I formed thee in the belly I knew thee; and before thou camest forth out of the womb I sanctified thee... (Jeremiah 1:5).

Can the Ethiopian change his skin, or the leopard his spots? then may ye also do good, that are accustomed to do evil (Jeremiah 13:23).

No conception is truly a mistake, and no birth is an accident. God is the One who determined and designed our bodies down to our sex, our race, and the minutest detail. Although some of us were conceived through acts of adultery, rape, or even incest, the fact is that ultimately it is the hand of sovereignty that determines which one of the multiple millions of sperm will hit the target and bring about conception. When we allow that truth to set in, it will free us from the prejudices we have toward people who are different from us.

No believer should have to alter his or her looks to be accepted and appreciated by other Christians. When we learn to accept and appreciate one another's God-given uniqueness, then the demons of racism, sexism, and discrimination will have no place to dwell among us!

6. Christian Employers or Managers Should Hire, Promote, or Dismiss People Based on Character and Competency, Not Race or Gender.

...He that ruleth over men must be just, ruling in the fear of God (2ⁿᵈ Samuel 23:3).

I charge thee before God, and the Lord Jesus Christ, and the elect angels, that thou observe these things without preferring one before another, doing nothing by partiality (1ˢᵗ Timothy 5:21).

Christians must resist racism in the workplace, and Christian employers and managers, in particular, must be fair and nondiscriminatory in their hiring, promoting, and firing polices. Recent research has uncovered a resurgence of racism, sexism, and discriminatory practices in the workplace, despite the quota system and affirmative action programs. This proves that racism and bigotry cannot be completely legislated away. I thank God for our Constitution and the Bill of Rights, but the law cannot alter human hearts and minds. Only the Word of God can demolish the attitudinal strongholds of racism and bigotry. The average Christian convert is not released from these erroneous racial attitudes at the initial stage of regeneration, but must be subsequently renewed and transformed in the mind (see Romans 12:2; Ephesians 4:23).

A true convert can be racist and prejudiced indefinitely if they fail to comply with the Word. Peter's racist behavior in Antioch (see Galatians 2:11-14), and the discriminatory treatment of the Grecian widows in Jerusalem (Acts 6:1) confirm this.

Christian employers and managers should take the lead in this war against racism by implementing nondiscriminatory policies and practices for hiring, firing, and promoting. You are a new creation now, and the world should not dictate your attitude or behavior. God's will is this: *"Do unto others as you would that they do unto you"* (adapted from Matthew 7:12).

7. Fellowship With Christians of Different Races and Cultures.

A man that hath friends must shew himself friendly: and there is a friend that sticketh closer than a brother (Proverbs 18:24).

And they continued stedfastly in the apostles' doctrine and fellowship, and in breaking of bread, and in prayers (Acts 2:42).

But if we walk in the light, as he is in the light, we have fellowship one with another, and the blood of Jesus Christ his Son cleanseth us from all sin (1st John 1:7).

Racism and segregation in the Church will quickly collapse when Christians and local churches begin to initiate fellowship with believers from other races, cultures, and nations. The pernicious viruses that cause racism—fear, ignorance, and racial superiority complexes—cannot survive in such a radiant and tranquil setting. If politicians can resolve their differences and formulate alliances upon common ground issues, how much more should we, who have the same Father, come together and create true friendships in spite of our ethnic differences?

8. Sponsor and Support Seminars and Symposiums on Racism.

But there rose up certain of the sect of the Pharisees which believed, saying, That it was needful to circumcise them, and to command them to keep the law of Moses. And the apostles and elders came together for to consider of this matter (Acts 15:5-6).

Where no counsel is, the people fall: but in the multitude of counsellors there is safety (Proverbs 11:14).

Come now, and let us reason together, saith the Lord... (Isaiah 1:18).

When diverse ethnic friendships and fellowships have been developed in the Church, racial problems can be effectively addressed and corrected through church-sponsored seminars and symposiums. Their objective should have nothing to do with debate, finger-pointing, or strife. Truth spoken in love will produce repentance, forgiveness, and healing.

According to the Book of Acts, "...the apostles and elders came together for to consider of this matter" (Acts 15:6). The issue was the Mosaic Law, and circumcision in particular. This meeting was possibly the first recorded seminar or symposium in Church history, and it provided an important scriptural precedent proving the value of joint counsel and discussion of controversial matters in the Church.

Since no one person possesses the sole expression of the mind of God, a more accurate picture can be produced in a "multitude of counselors." The Hebrew word translated as *safety* in Proverbs 11:14 is *teshuah*. The same Hebrew word is translated in many other places in the Bible as *deliverance*. The support or sponsorship of seminars and symposiums on controversial issues in the Church is a *Divine strategy* that yields *deliverance*.

God declared to man, "Come now, and let us reason together..." (Isaiah 1:18). Although Isaiah was delivering God's invitation to a backslidden Judah to repent and be reconciled with Him, this verse also reveals a divine principle that will devastate racist concepts and attitudes in the Church! Most of our animosity and racial division will begin to dissolve immediately when our church leaders agree to reason together, regardless of their ethnicity. I pray that some Christian "gladiators" will read this material and be inspired by God to initiate a forum to destroy the dragon of racism.

9. Submit to the Holy Spirit if He Impresses You to Join a Church Pastored by Someone of a Different Race.

And I will give you pastors according to mine heart, which shall feed you with knowledge and understanding (Jeremiah 3:15).

There is neither Jew nor Greek, there is neither bond nor free, there is neither male nor female: for ye are all one in Christ Jesus (Galatians 3:28).

We must integrate believers of various races into the local church if racism is to be eradicated from the Church. I'm not talking about some integration policy forced on church members by an ecclesiastical hierarchy. We should encourage believers who are sensitive, submissive, and courageous enough to join local churches that are pastored and populated by a majority of believers from a different race or culture.

Over the years, it has become more common to see African-American faces scattered throughout predominantly Caucasian churches, but the opposite situation is not as common. There are some very renowned and competent African-American pastors whose ministries and churches are comparable to those of Caucasian pastors (including Fred Price, Charles E. Blake, Tony Evans, T. D. Jakes and Creflo Dollar). Yet the same ratio of Caucasian believers in their congregation does not compare to the influx of African-Americans who have joined such notable Caucasian ministers as Rod Parsley, John Hagee, Benny Hinn, Jim Cymbala, and a host of others. I rejoice over the ministries of these great men of God, but the uneven race ratio reveals a lack of internalization of the Word of God leading to visible demonstrations of racism in the Church.

Perhaps some Caucasians find it difficult to join predominantly African-American congregations led by African-American leadership because African-American men have been stereotyped for centuries as incompetent, irresponsible, and ignorant in comparison to their Caucasian counterparts.

The first Caucasian family to join our predominately African-American congregation had to contend with the reality of racism in their lives and in the community. Having come from New England and in a sparsely integrated predominately Caucasian church, they felt sure that they could further integrate our fellowship by their testimonies and example.

Things seemed to go well for a while. Then it happened! This once determined Caucasian couple that said God had led them to our fellowship, began to draw back and avoid us in public. The subtle yet pervasive racism in our rural Southern town aggravated the small seed of racism within them. They had failed to count the cost of confronting racism in the community, and they hadn't removed the seed of racism in their hearts before attempting to expose it in others. Now I could be wrong, but I believe that if I was Caucasian, they would have fought much harder to remain a part of our fellowship (in spite of the predominately African-American congregation).

An African-American friend of mine assumed the pastoral position for a discredited Caucasian minister in a nearby town. When he was installed as pastor of this integrated church where Caucasian members were the majority, he was amazed and disappointed to see most of the Caucasian parishioners leave the fold because they could not be subordinate to a African-American man!

Unfortunately, this is not an isolated incident in the Christian community. I have come across several similar incidents in my research. If the Church is to be truly desegregated and racism annihilated, then more Caucasian believers must dare to do what many African-American brethren have been doing for some time—they must be willing to join predominantly African-American congregation as African-American believers have done with predominately Caucasian churches.

When courageous Caucasian believers under the leading of God begin to pull down the stronghold of racial superiority and pride and willfully submit under the authority of African-American pastors in churches that are predominately African-American, racism will be shattered.

10. Do Not Support Churches or Organizations That Practice Racism.

The word of the Lord also came unto me, saying, Son of man, thou dwellest in the midst of a rebellious house, which have eyes to see, and see not; they have ears to hear, and hear not: for they are a rebellious house Therefore, thou son of man, prepare thee stuff for removing, and remove by day in their sight; and thou shalt remove from thy place to another place in their sight: it may be they will consider, though they be a rebellious house (Ezekiel 12:1-3).

But now I have written unto you not to keep company, if any man that is called a brother be a fornicator, or covetous, or an idolater, or a railer, or a drunkard, or an extortioner; with such an one no not to eat (1st Corinthians 5:11).

Wherefore come out from among them, and be ye separate, saith the Lord, and touch not the unclean thing; and I will receive you. And will be a Father unto you, and ye shall be my sons and daughters, saith the Lord Almighty (2nd Corinthians 6:17-18).

At what point should we protest against the overt racial policies of our church or group? Would you remain in a group or ministry that openly advocated adultery, theft, or deception?

The recent demise or decline of some popular televangelistic ministries and megachurches confirms that the Christian community as a whole will no longer blindly support or tolerate compromises of integrity or morality. Shouldn't the same thing hold true for churches and groups who condone the sin of racism?

Many Christian so deeply abhor abortion and homosexuality that they are willing to go to the streets in protest, yet they refuse to confront the racism in their churches. There should be a widespread and constant outcry against the sin racism, just as we publicly protest other prominent sins (see 1st John 5:17).

I commend the Church's strong public stand against abortion and homosexuality (while loving the sinners). However, we should treat racism the same way we treat other sins. God classes racism—the hatred of other men and women—in the same class as adultery, theft, murder, deception, or any other work of the flesh. To Him they all spell sin. He instructs us to not "keep company" with any so called brother in Christ who is "a fornicator, or covetous, or an idolator, or a railer, or a drunkard, or an extortioner." The same principle holds true for those so-called brothers who advocate and promote racism.

Any Christian who supports any church or group that knowingly promotes racism is without excuse and stands guilty before God!

If I had not come and spoken unto them, they had not

had sin: but now they have no cloak [excuse] for their sin (John 15:22).

Lay hands suddenly on no man, neither be partaker of other men's sins: keep thyself pure (1st Timothy 5:22).

11. Intercede for All Leaders in Regard to Racial Harmony in the Church.

If My people, which are called by My name, shall humble themselves, and pray, and seek My face, and turn from their wicked ways; then will I hear from heaven, and will forgive their sin, and will heal their land (2nd Chronicles 7:14).

I exhort therefore, that, first of all, supplications, prayers, intercessions, and giving of thanks, be made for all men; for kings, and for all that are in authority... (1st Timothy 2:1-2).

It is impossible to achieve healing and victory over racism in the Church without the aid of prayer. Healing for the wound that separates us can only come through unified prayer to God who makes us one! The devil and his cohorts are the unseen instigators of the racial animosity in the Church. Since the ancient campaign of racism is not natural, we must fight this war through prayer and spiritual warfare. The strongholds of racism cannot be demolished merely through great teaching, preaching, or reasoning. The god of this world has blinded the minds of people (see 2nd Corinthians 4:4), so racism can only be destroyed by prayer and fasting.

> *Is not this the fast that I have chosen? to loose the bands of wickedness, to undo the heavy burdens, and to let the oppressed go free, and that ye break every yoke? Is it not to deal thy bread to the hungry, and that thou bring the poor that are cast out to thy house? when thou seest the naked, that thou cover him; and that thou hide not thyself from thine own flesh? Then shall thy light break forth as the morning, and thine health shall spring forth speedily: and thy righteousness shall go before thee; the glory of the Lord shall be thy rereward* (Isaiah 58:6-8).

The eighth verse reveals the fruit of the battle against racism. When we intercede for Christian leaders, something supernatural happens. If the great Apostle Paul needed and asked for prayer, how much more do contemporary Christian leaders need it?

> *Praying always with all prayer and supplication in the Spirit, and watching thereunto with all perseverance and supplication for all saints; and for me, that utterance may be given unto me, that I may open my mouth boldly, to make known the mystery of the gospel, for which I am an ambassador in bonds: that therein I may speak boldly, as I ought to speak* (Ephesians 6:18-20).

> *Finally, brethren, pray for us, that the word of the Lord may have free course, and be glorified, even as it is with you: and that we may be delivered from unreasonable and wicked men: for all men have not faith* (2nd Thessalonians 3:1-2).

Prayer and intercession are crucial if we are to uproot and destroy racism in the Church. I encourage you to stand in the gap for spiritual leaders everywhere, regardless of their convictions or racial policies. Even if they are narrow-minded bigots, James assures us that our effectual fervent prayers will ultimately prevail (see James 5:16-20).

12. Forgive Everyone Who Has Hurt You Through Their Racism.

And forgive us our debts, as we forgive our debtors. ... For if ye forgive men their trespasses, your heavenly Father will also forgive you: but if ye forgive not men their trespasses, neither will your Father forgive your trespasses (Matthew 6:12,14-15).

Then came Peter to him, and said, Lord, how oft shall my brother sin against me, and I forgive him? till seven times? Jesus saith unto him, I say not unto thee, Until seven times: but, Until seventy times seven (Matthew 18:21-22).

What is the role of forgiveness in the healing process? The malignancy of racism has inflicted many wounds and scars on the lives of Christians—both African-Americans and Caucasians. It has terribly disfigured and divided the Body of Christ in the process. Nevertheless, I am encouraged and optimistic because I know that our Lord is coming back for a unified and glorious Church without blemish (see Ephesians 5:27). We must be willing to forgive those who have hurt or offended us through racism and bigotry before healing can begin in the Church. This applies to all Christians, but it is especially true for African-American believers. No other ethnic group in America has been so victimized by systematic racism, bigotry, and slavery. We must be willing to forgive, no matter how deep or severe our wounds may be.

An atmosphere of anger and animosity attempted to settle upon our congregation (especially the young people) after they watched a documentary on the Civil Rights struggle. Prompted by the Holy Spirit, our youth pastor quickly quoted the Scripture,

> *"Wherefore, my beloved brethren, let every man be swift to hear, slow to speak, slow to wrath: for the wrath of man worketh not the righteousness of God" (James 1:19-20).*

After the emotional crisis was defused, the youth pastor began to describe the effectiveness of the nonviolent strategy of Dr. Martin Luther King Jr. in comparison to the vengeful eye-for-an-eye tactics of men like Malcolm X and Stokely Carmichael. History has acclaimed Dr. King's way as the more excellent way. When you consider the achievements of this apostle of Civil Rights and his comrades through their nonviolent and conciliatory efforts, you have to conclude that God was not only their ally, but also the architect of their strategy!

We must embrace a similar strategy and be forgiving if we are to overcome the demons of racism and bigotry in the Church today. God will not fight our battles or forgive our sins unless we are willing to forgive others—whether they repent or not. The moment we fail to practice unconditional forgiveness toward others is the moment God stops forgiving us.

> *And when ye stand praying, forgive, if ye have ought against any: that your Father also which is in heaven may forgive you your trespasses (Mark 11:25).*

Put on therefore, as the elect of God, holy and beloved, bowels of mercies, kindness, humbleness of mind, meekness, longsuffering; forbearing one another, and forgiving one another, if any man have a quarrel against any: even as Christ forgave you, so also do ye. And above all these things put on charity, which is the bond of perfectness (Colossians 3:12-14).

Final Words

If this book has enlightened, blessed, or transformed you in regard to racism in the Church, then pass it on to someone else or purchase one as a gift to give. The disease of racism is invading the Church family, and it is too serious to ignore or sweep under the rug of religious indifference.

God is demanding that the Church acknowledge her sin and rise up to rid herself of this deadly evil. There are no neutral bystanders in this struggle. You and I can either be part of the problem or part of the solution! Since God has declared His position, He is forcing us to choose. Will we stand with God and oppose racism wherever we find it, or will we stand apart from Him apart from His blessings?

Since you took the trouble to read this book, I feel I already know your answer. It is time to get busy. There is a worldwide family of grace to embrace and unite in Christ!

End Notes

1. *"With God There Is No Color Lines,"* Charisma (September 1990), p.132

2. John Gimenez, *God the Boxer* (Shippensburg, PA: Destiny Image Publishers, 1993), p.17

3. *A Testament of Hope: The Essential Writings & Speeches of Martin Luther King, Jr.* (New York, NY: Harper Collins Publishers, 1986), p.479.

4. *American Heritage Dictionary,* Second College Edition (Boston, MA: Houghton Mifflin Company, 1985), p.1020.

5. Adapted from the article, *"The Founding of Black America,"* by Lerone Bennett, Jr., Ebony magazine (February 1992), pp.108-116.

6. Finis Jennings Dake, *Dake's Anotated Reference Bible,* "Notes on the Book of Acts" (Lawrenceville, GA: Dake Bible Sales, Inc.), p.159.

About the Author

Bishop Michael Goings is a lifelong resident of Dillon, South Carolina, where he was born and raised. He is the founder and pastor of Outreach Family Fellowship in Dillon and Florence, South Carolina, as well as the founder and co-founder of several other churches. He is the Apostle and Prelate of the Fellowship of International Churches (F.O.I.C.), where he serves as Bishop and counselor to many pastors. He is a prolific writer and author of several published books that have made an impact on the Body of Christ. He is also a historian for over forty years. Bishop Goings attended the American International College in Springfield, Massachusetts and served three years in the Army. He credits this brief stint in the military as his "boot camp" for life. Bishop Goings' main hobbies, besides his addiction to reading and watching old westerns and the military channel, are his daily morning rides with his pal, Nip the pug, by his side. He travels extensively throughout America, as well as abroad, conducting conferences and seminars in regards to biblical and theological issues. He holds many awards and citations from the state of South Carolina. He is also the recipient of an Honorary Doctor's Degree in Theology from Cathedral Bible College.

Bishop Goings is married to Dr. Louise Goings, who is an educator. They have two adult children -- Jennifer (who is married) and Michael.

Bishop Goings is a man who leads by example in commitment, integrity, and most of all prayer.

Bishop Goings is available to any church or group who wishes to have him come and minister during a conference, seminar, etc. All correspondence should be sent:

Bishop Michael Goings
401 Pee Dee Church Road, Dillon, SC 29536
Office: (803) 774-0928, Home: (803) 774-8512

www.ingramcontent.com/pod-product-compliance
Lightning Source LLC
Chambersburg PA
CBHW050437010526
44118CB00013B/1568